To
James and Emily

Wine and Food with
laughter are the best
ingredients

Sylvia Sebastiani
1988

The Sebastiani FAMILY COOKBOOK

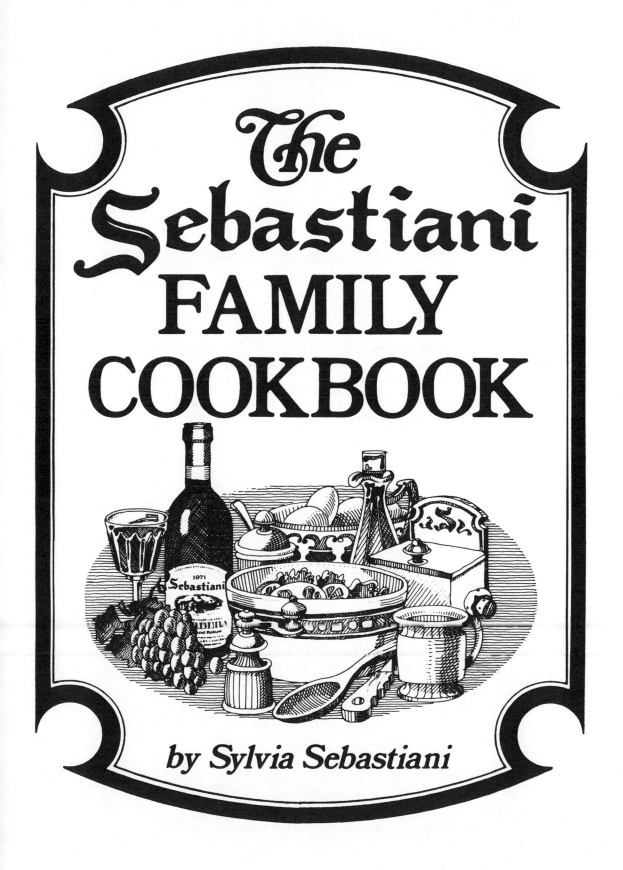

by Sylvia Sebastiani

Eighth printing

Library of Congress Cataloging in Publication Data

Sebastiani, Sylvia.
    The Sebastiani family cookbook.

    Published in 1970 under title: Mangiamo (let's eat!)
    1. Cooking, Italian. I. Title.
TX723.S37 1977   641.5'945   76-30276
ISBN 0-8184-0244-X

Artwork by
EARLE P. BROWN
Our dear friend and woodcarver who produced over
300 carvings on doors and wine casks at Sebastiani Vineyards

Contents

Sylvia Sebastiani at work in her kitchen.

FOREWORD

The following pages are a result of the many requests of my family and friends for recipes which they have enjoyed in my home. It is my desire that this book will help you to enjoy these dishes as they do.

I express sincere gratitude to Colonel Paul Walker. Had it not been for his patience, effort and advice in editing, I am sure this book would never have been completed.

To those relatives and friends from whom I have acquired a number of these recipes, I give a special thanks.

May you have many pleasurable cooking experiences!

Sylvia Sebasteanu

INTRODUCTION

Reading through *The Sylvia Sebastiani Cookbook,* I became ravenously hungry—and astonished with her vast repertoire of old-world and modern recipes. Not only are there refreshingly creative variations on familiar dishes, but there are marvelous unusual treats, ranging from Aunt Mary's biscotti to Sylvia's own butter-ball soup. The recipes read swiftly—as good recipes should. And Sylvia's excellent suggestions for cooking meats, vegetables, soups, desserts are based on her long experience of being one of the California wine country's best cooks—she offers tips about how to remove a cake from a sticky pan, how to cut cookie-baking time in half, how to keep rice grains separated, how to make rice whiter, along with countless other knowledgeable pointers.

Sylvia is a kitchen wizard, which I knew before I read her book; and now, thankfully, the whole world will know it. I can't imagine a better gift for anyone who likes food, since Sylvia's collection of recipes includes some of the best Italian-oriented "wine country cookery" that I have come across. And, if I may make a suggestion, it makes sense, doesn't it, to accompany Sylvia's dishes with the various fine wines of Sebastiani Vineyards.

GEORGE CHRISTY

Author & Columnist
Specializing in Food & Wine

Beverages

Champagne Punch

2   bottles August Sebastiani
Champagne
1   13½ oz. can pineapple chunks
or crushed pineapple
2   cans frozen pink lemonade, thawed
1   large bottle soda
½   cup maraschino cherry syrup

Combine all ingredients and chill well. Serves about 15 people.

Fruit and Brandy Drink

1   pint brandy
juice of 3 oranges
juice of 3 lemons
1   small can pineapple tidbits
1   large bottle 7-Up
sugar to taste

Mix all ingredients and chill well. Serve in punch cups. Serves 12-15.

Gin and Champagne Punch

1   bottle August Sebastiani
Champagne or Sebastiani
Brut Three-Star.
6   liters August Sebastiani
Chablis
1   quart gin
½   pint lemon juice
½   pint grapefruit juice
1   quart pineapple juice
sugar to taste

Combine all ingredients, adding sugar to taste. Chill well. Serves about 25 people.

Hot Buttered Rum

1   lb. brown sugar
¼   lb. butter
½   teaspoon nutmeg
½   teaspoon cinnamon
½   teaspoon cloves (ground)
pinch of salt
1½   ozs. rum for each serving
hot water

Cream sugar and butter until smooth. Add nutmeg, cinnamon, cloves, and salt. Preheat a 6 oz. mug. Drop a heaping teaspoon of batter into mug, add 1½ ozs. rum, and fill with hot water. Should serve 12 people.

Tom and Jerry

6   eggs, separated
1   lb. superfine granulated sugar
½   teaspoon baking soda
½   oz. rum for each serving
½   oz. brandy for each serving
     hot milk, hot water, or hot coffee
     nutmeg

In electric mixer, beat egg yolks until lemon-colored. Add sugar very slowly, taking 10-15 minutes or longer. Beat well. Fold in stiffly-beaten egg whites and mix well. Add baking soda and blend well. Continue beating for 10-15 minutes or more; the longer the batter is mixed, the better it will hold together. In a heavy mug, place 1 spoon of batter plus ½ oz. rum and ½ oz. brandy. Fill cup with milk, water or coffee, stir well, fleck with nutmeg, and serve.

I usually keep the batter in the electric mixer bowl so that if it separates, I can combine it simply by re-beating.

Mulled Wine

1½   cups boiling water
½   cup fine granulated sugar
     rind of 1 lemon
1   2 inch stick of cinnamon
10   cloves
1   1.5 liter bottle August Sebastiani Burgundy or Country Pinot Noir
     marshmallow (optional)
     nutmeg

Boil water, sugar, lemon rind, cinnamon, and cloves for about 15 minutes. Heat wine separately, but do not boil. Add to water mixture and strain. Serve in cups. Fleck with nutmeg and garnish with a marshmallow stuck on a toothpick, if desired. Serves 10-12.

This is a wonderful wintertime or Holiday drink!

Champagne Cooler

2   6 oz. cans frozen lemonade
2   6 oz. cans frozen orange juice
1   quart soda, well-chilled
2   bottles August Sebastiani Champagne
1   quart lemon sherbert

In a large chilled bowl, combine frozen juices with soda. Stir in champagne, then add sherbet. Serves about 20 people.

Port Wine Cocktail

2   eggs
2   teaspoons powdered sugar
1   cup Tawny Port
½ cup brandy
    cracked ice

Break eggs into a shaker glass. Add sugar, Port, brandy, and ice. Shake well. Strain and serve. Serves 4-6.

Rosé Punch

1   **1.5 liter bottle August Sebastiani Vin Rosé or Country White Zinfandel**
¼ **bottle Dry Sherry**
¼ **bottle Tawny Port**
    juice of 1 small lemon
1   **small bottle 7-Up**
1   **18 oz. can sweetened pineapple juice**
½ **cup Karo syrup**

Mix all ingredients together and chill. Serve in punch bowl over ice block. Serves 20-25.

Vintage Julep

1 sprig of mint
2 tablespoons Karo syrup
3 teaspoons maraschino cherry juice
2 teaspoons lemon juice
2 ice cubes
   Sebastiani Chenin Blanc or August
   Sebastiani Country French
   Colombard

In a highball glass, mull mint sprig in syrup. Add cherry juice and lemon juice, stirring well. Add ice cubes and fill with wine. Makes 1 highball.

Wine Party Punch

1   pint Tawny Port
½   pint brandy
1   pint Dry Sherry
3   pints ginger ale
½   pint sugar syrup (½ cup sugar
     melted over low heat with a small
     amount of water)
3   lemons or 2 oranges, thinly sliced
2   bottles August Sebastiani
     Champagne or Sebastiani
     Brut Three-Star

Combine all ingredients, except champagne, in a large punch bowl with a block of ice. Just prior to serving, add champagne. Serves 20-25.

Sensation Punch

2   bottles August Sebastiani
     Champagne or Sebastiani Brut
     Three-Star
5   ozs. brandy
5   ozs. Cointreau Liqueur
5   dashes lemon juice
     strawberries or raspberries
     (optional)

Mix all ingredients just before serving time in a punch bowl with a block of ice. Add berries, if desired. Serves about 15.

Sherry Manhattan

1   bottle Dry Sherry
1   bottle Sweet Vermouth
4   tablespoons maraschino cherry
     juice

Combine all ingredients and chill well. Serves 20-25.

This is the basic recipe, but you can vary any of the ingredients to suit your taste. Some like a few drops of bitters added or a sliced whole orange.

Hors d'
Oeuvres

Anchovy Puffs

1 3 oz. package cream cheese
1 cube butter, softened
1 cup flour
1 2 oz. tube anchovy paste

Mix cheese, butter, and flour well together until it forms a smooth dough. Roll very thin on floured board and cut into 2 inch rounds with a biscuit cutter or glass. Place about ¼ teaspoon of anchovy paste in center of each round and press together with fingers to form a turnover. Bake in 350 degree oven until slightly brown, about 10 minutes.

Antipasto

6 small artichokes, trimmed and cut in half
1 small bunch carrots
1 celery heart, cut up small
½ lb. string beans, cut up small
1 quart white vinegar
1 quart water
½ lb. peas, fresh or frozen
1 small cauliflower, broken in small pieces
1 lb. small white onions
6 small sweet pickles, drained
1 small jar green olives, drained
1 small can tomato juice
1 cup olive oil
1 small can button mushrooms, drained
1 large can chunk tuna, packed in olive oil
½ lb. small wax peppers
   salt, pepper to taste

Boil artichokes, carrots, celery, and beans for 10 minutes in vinegar and water. Add peas, cauliflower, onions, pickles, and olives and boil for 15 minutes longer. Drain when cooked. Boil tomato juice, oil, and mushrooms. Add drained ingredients to this and let come to a good rolling boil. Salt and pepper to taste. Put into jars along with 1 wax pepper and a piece of tuna. Seal tightly.

May be kept in refrigerator several weeks if desired.

Artichoke Frittata

3   6 oz. jars marinated artichoke hearts
    chopped
    oil from artichoke hearts
3   bunches green onions, chopped
1   clove garlic, chopped
8   eggs
10 soda crackers, crumbled
½   bunch parsley, chopped
1   lb. wedge Wispride cheddar cheese
    dash Tabasco sauce
    dash Worcestershire sauce
    salt, pepper to taste

Put oil from artichoke hearts in pan. Fry onions and garlic until limp. Beat eggs in bowl; add crumbs, and beat again. Add parsley, cheese, Tabasco, Worcestershire, and artichokes, beating well after each addition. Season with salt and pepper to taste. When well-blended, put in oiled 8 x 12 pan and bake at 325 degrees for 35 minutes until firm. Let cool. Cut into strips and wrap each strip separately in Saran wrap and freeze. When ready to serve, thaw and cut into 1 inch squares. Can also be served hot if you like.

Baby Puffs

1   cup boiling water
½   cup butter
½   teaspoon salt
1   cup flour
4   eggs

Put water into top of double boiler and boil at medium heat. Add butter and salt; boil until all butter is melted. Put flour in water all at once and reduce heat to low. Stir until mixture leaves sides of pan and coats spoon. Remove from heat and let cool 5 minutes. Break 1 egg at a time into cooled mixture, beating well after each addition until dough gets shiny. Place dough by level teaspoonfuls onto greased cookie sheets. Bake at 400 degrees for 10 minutes, then reduce heat to 350 degrees and let cook for 20 minutes. Turn oven off, let puffs stand in oven with door open for 15 minutes. (This dries the shells out.) Makes about 60 shells which can be filled with your favorite spread or dip.

This recipe for baby puffs can also be used for making cream puff shells with the following variations.
1. Place dough on cookie sheet by tablespoonfuls
2. Bake at 450 degrees for 20 minutes. Reduce heat to 350 and bake for 20 minutes.
3. Turn oven off, let shells stand in oven with door open for 15 minutes. Makes 12 shells.
4. See crab filling for baby puffs in this section.

Crab Filling for Baby Puffs

1 cup fresh crab meat or
   1 large can crabmeat, chopped fine
¼ cup chopped parsley
½ cup tender celery, chopped fine
1 tablespoon white vinegar
2 tablespoons mayonnaise
½ teaspoon beau monde seasoning
   white pepper to taste

Mix all ingredients together and stuff into baby puff shells.

Prosciutto and Bread Sticks

prosciutto, very thinly sliced
bread sticks, 4 inches long

Cut prosciutto into 1-1½ inch strips and wrap around individual bread sticks. Serve as is.

Dipped Bread Cubes

1 large loaf of stale sandwich
   bread, unsliced
2 cubes butter
2 jars Old English sharp cheddar cheese
   slivered almonds or pine nuts

Trim all crust from bread and cut bread into 1½ inch cubes. Cook butter and cheese together in top of double boiler. Dip bread cubes into this mixture and freeze immediately. Prior to serving heat in 350 degree oven 10-15 minutes. Place 2-3 almond slivers or pine nuts on top of each cube.

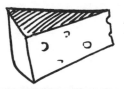

Rosa Angelina's Hot Mexican Cheese Dip

2 lbs. Kraft Velveeta cheese
1 can cheddar cheese soup
1 10 oz. can chilies and tomatoes,
   chopped
1 teaspoon garlic salt
1 teaspoon onion salt
1 teaspoon Salsa Jalapena

Cube Velveeta and melt in top of double boiler. Add soup and tomatoes and blend. Add garlic salt, onion salt, and Salsa Jalapena, stirring well. Use tortilla triangles to dip.

Salsa Jalapena, a commercially-prepared sauce, is very hot, so use your own judgment as to quantity.

Canteloupe Cubes

8   slices proscuitto
1   medium size canteloupe

Cut proscuitto into 1 in. strips. Cut canteloupe into cubes. Wrap strips of prosciutto around each canteloupe cube and secure with toothpick. Serve chilled.

For another variation, use smoked salmon strips and wrap around cubes of honeydew melon. When melons are out of season, use cubes of avocado or papaya and top with a sprinkling of black pepper.

Clam Dip

2   cans minced clams
½   cup clam juice
4   jars Borden's cheddar cheese very sharp
¾   bunch green onions, chopped
1   small clove garlic, chopped
6   shakes paprika
1   tablespoon Worcestershire sauce
6   shakes Tabasco sauce
5   tablespoons chopped parsley

Blend all ingredients together and bake in uncovered casserole for 20 minutes at 350 degrees. Reduce heat to 200 degrees and let bake for 45 minutes. Serve in chafing dish. Toasted bread, crackers, or melba toast are excellent with this dip.

Crab or Shrimp Dip

3   8 oz. packages cream cheese
3   large cans king crab
     dash garlic salt
½   cup mayonnaise
2   teaspoons prepared mustard
1   teaspoon dry mustard
1   tablespoon lemon juice
¼   cup August Sebastiani Chablis or Country Chenin Blanc
2   teaspoons powdered sugar
1   teaspoon onion juice
     dash of salt
2   dashes cayenne pepper

Melt cream cheese in top of double boiler. Add remaining ingredients and mix well. May be served hot or cold. Also freezes quite well.

Hot Crab Cheese Spread

1   8 oz. package cream cheese
1   tablespoon light cream
2   teaspoons Worcestershire sauce
1   teaspoon lemon juice
    dash of cayenne pepper
1   7½ oz. can crabmeat
2   tablespoons green onion, chopped
    toasted slivered almonds

Combine cheese, cream, Worcestershire, lemon juice, and cayenne. Drain crab and wash thoroughly with cold running water. Drain again. Add crab and onion to cheese mixture. Turn mixture into a buttered shallow baking pan and sprinkle with almonds. Bake at 350 degrees for 15 minutes. (Can be frozen if you wish.)

Bleu Cheese Balls

1½ lbs. bleu cheese
1   8 oz. package cream cheese
1   cube soft butter
1   small onion, chopped fine
1   clove garlic, minced
    cayenne pepper to taste
4   tablespoons Sebastiani Chenin
    Blanc or "Eye of the Swan"
    Pinot Noir Blanc

Let cheeses and butter warm to room temperature, then beat together until light and well-blended. Add onion, garlic, pepper, and sherry. Chill until manageable to roll in balls. After forming balls, roll them in nuts until well covered. Place on a tray with your favorite crackers.

Olive-Cheese Balls

1   cup grated sharp Cheddar cheese
2   tablespoons butter
½   cup flour
    dash of cayenne pepper
1   clove garlic, pressed (optional)
    salt, pepper to taste
25 medium olives, well-drained,
    either black or green (pitted)

Cream cheese and butter together. Add flour, pepper, garlic, and salt and pepper to taste. Wrap a teaspoonful of this mixture around each olive making a ball. Bake for 15 minutes at 400 degrees. Serve with cocktail picks.

Minced Clam Canapes

    approximately 36 bread rounds, 1¾
    inch in diameter
1   8 oz. package cream cheese
1   tablespoon Worcestershire sauce
2-3 dashes cayenne pepper
¼   teaspoon salt
2   teaspoons grated onion
1   can minced clams, drained well
    grated Parmesan cheese
    paprika

Toast bread rounds on 1 side. Cream cheese with Worcestershire, cayenne, salt, onion, and clams. Heap by teaspoons on untoasted side of bread rounds. Sprinkle over with cheese and paprika. Place under broiler half way down in oven so that they will cook and brown slowly. Broil until lightly brown, about 5 minutes and serve hot. Makes about 3 dozen.

11

Crabmeat Canapes

3   tablespoons butter
3   tablespoons flour
½   cup cream
¼   cup chicken stock
¼   cup August Sebastiani Chablis or
    Country Chardonnay
2   tablespoons minced parsley
1   teaspoon minced onion
1   cup crabmeat, fresh or canned
    salt, garlic salt, pepper to taste
60 1½ inch rounds of white bread
    grated Parmesan cheese
    paprika

Melt butter and stir in flour. Add cream and chicken stock. Cook, stirring constantly, until thick. Remove from heat and add wine, parsley, onion, crab, and seasonings to taste. Chill thoroughly. Toast rounds of bread on cookie sheet, only on 1 side. Spread untoasted side with crab mixture. Sprinkle with cheese and paprika. Broil until browned. Serve at once.

Rolled Sandwiches

1   8 ounce package cream cheese
4-6 tablespoons soft butter
2-4 tablespoons white vinegar (distilled)
¼   cup parsley (chopped fine)
     salt and white pepper to taste
     lemon pepper (optional)

1   loaf (fresh) sliced sandwich bread
     crusts removed.

Cream cheese and butter together, add vinegar and seasonings and mix well. Take 3 slices of bread, overlap each slice about one half inch and roll with a rolling pin so that one long sheet of bread is formed. Spread cream cheese mixture over bread and roll. Wrap roll in wax paper and twist at each end. Chill or freeze overnight. When ready to serve cut into about ¼ inch slices. If bread rolls have been frozen allow to thaw before slicing.

You can use your imagination with these cold sandwiches. Leftover chicken, chopped fine or hot dogs can be used, also caviar. Simply mix the meat or caviar with the cream cheese mixture. Sweet pickles or stuffed green olives can be placed at one end of the bread before you start the roll.

Bacon and Onion Spread

1	lb. bacon
6	green onions
5	tablespoons mayonnaise
4	English muffins, halves

Fry bacon until crisp. Then chop fine. Mince green onions and add to bacon, along with mayonnaise. Brown muffin halves, then spread with bacon mixture. Toast in 350 degree oven for 10 minutes. Cut each half into quarters and serve. If desired, spread can be used on crackers directly, without toasting.

Bacon and Water Chestnuts

1	5 oz. can water chestnuts, drained
¼	cup soy sauce
¼	cup sugar
6-8	slices bacon, cut in ½ lengthwise and cut in 3 pieces crosswise

Marinate water chestnuts in soy sauce for 45 minutes. Roll each chestnut in sugar, wrap with a piece of bacon and secure with a toothpick. Arrange on broiler pan and bake for 20 minutes at 400 degrees. Drain well before serving. Serve hot.

Bagna Cauda

4	celery stalks, cut into strips
2	carrots, cut into strips
1	green pepper, cut into strips
¼	lb. fresh mushrooms, cut into quarters if large
	Italian bread sticks
1	cup heavy cream
4	tablespoons butter
1	2 oz. can anchovy filets, drained and chopped fine
1	clove garlic, pressed

Clean and soak vegetables about an hour to crisp them. Arrange on platter along with mushrooms and bread sticks. In a heavy saucepan, bring the cream to a boil and stir frequently until thick. In a flameproof casserole, melt butter over low heat, but do not brown. Add anchovies, garlic, and thickened cream. Do not boil. Serve at once with platter of vegetables, mushrooms, and bread sticks.

Any vegetables of your choice may be used with this dip.

Champagne Bleu Cheese Spread

½	lb. bleu cheese
½	lb. butter
	cayenne pepper to taste
½	cup August Sebastiani Champagne or Sebastiani Brut
¼	cup brandy

Blend cheese, butter, and cayenne into a smooth paste. Moisten with champagne and brandy and serve with crackers or any good bread.

Eggs Stuffed with Chicken

6   hard-cooked eggs
¼   cup cooked chicken, chopped fine
3   teaspoons mayonnaise
2   teaspoons white vinegar
½   teaspoon prepared mustard
     dash of cayenne pepper
     salt, garlic salt to taste
     mayonnaise
     parsley
     paprika

Halve eggs and mash yolks with chicken. Add mayonnaise, vinegar mustard, cayenne, salt, and garlic salt, adding more mayonnaise if necessary to attain creamy texture. Fill egg whites and garnish each with a dot of mayonnaise and a sprinkling each of parsley and paprika.

Stuffed French Rolls

1   lb. salami, ground or chopped fine
2   jars creamy sharp cheddar spread
¼-½   cup August Sebastiani Country
       Zinfandel
6-8   sour French rolls

Mix salami, cheese spread, and wine together. With a knife, take centers out of French rolls and stuff with salami mixture. Chill overnight and slice before serving.

Broiled Stuffed Mushrooms

1   lb. mushrooms
2 or 3 green onions, chopped fine
3   tablespoons butter
¼   cup bread crumbs
¼   cup chopped parsley
¼   teaspoon oregano
¼   teaspoon salt
       few grains cayenne pepper
3   tablespoons grated Parmesan cheese
2   teaspoons Sebastiani Chardonnay
       paprika

Wash mushrooms and drain well. Remove stems and chop fine along with onion; then sauté together lightly in butter. Add remaining ingredients and heat until warm. Brush mushroom caps lightly with butter or oil. Press stuffing into caps, sprinkle over with paprika, and heat under broiler until mushrooms are tender, about 5 minutes.

Meat Balls

¾ lb. ground beef
¼ lb. ground pork
¼ cup soft bread crumbs
1 egg
2 tablespoons grated onion
1 teaspoon lemon juice
½ teaspoon salt
½ teaspoon pepper
½ teaspoon Accent
½ cup applesauce
½ cup water
½ cup ketchup

Mix beef, pork, bread crumbs, egg, onion, lemon juice, and seasonings. Blend well and form into ½ inch balls. Brown meat balls in a little oil; add applesauce, water and ketchup. Pour into greased baking dish and bake ½ hour at 350 degrees. Place into chafing dish to keep warm while serving. Serves 6-8.

Stuffed Belgian Endive

1 cup cooked shrimp or crab
¼ cup mayonnaise
¼ teaspoon dry mustard
1 teaspoon white vinegar
  salt, white pepper, beau monde
  seasoning to taste
  dash of cayenne pepper
1 head Belgian lettuce

Combine shrimp or crab with mayonnaise and vinegar and season to taste with salt, white pepper, and beau monde seasoning, adding a dash of cayenne pepper at the end. Place 1 teaspoon of this mixture at base of each endive leaf. Arrange on a platter and serve as appetizers.

For an interesting variation, cooked artichoke leaves may be used instead of the Belgian endive.

Stuffed Eggs

6 hard-cooked eggs
4 tablespoons soft butter
3 tablespoons mayonnaise
2 teaspoons minced onion
1 teaspoon prepared mustard
½ teaspoon white vinegar
1 teaspoon garlic salt
  dash of cayenne pepper
  mayonnaise
  parsley sprigs

Halve eggs and mash yolks with fork. Mix them with butter, mayonnaise, onion, mustard, vinegar, and seasonings. Fill egg whites, garnish with a dab of mayonnaise and tiny sprig of parsley on top of each half.

Shrimp Mousse

1   **envelope unflavored gelatine**
¼   **cup cold water**
¾   **cup Sebastiani Sauvignon Blanc**
1   **7 oz. can shrimp**
1   **tablespoon chopped onion**
1   **teaspoon lemon juice**
½   **teaspoon dry mustard**
1   **cup mayonnaise**
    salt, white pepper to taste
    dash of cayenne pepper
    several lettuce leaves
    few sprigs parsley (optional)
    lemon peel (optional)

Soften gelatine in water. Heat wine and stir in gelatine until dissolved. Let cool thoroughly. Put shrimp, onion, lemon juice, mustard, and seasonings in blender; add mayonnaise last and mix until smooth. Stir in cooled wine mixture and pour into mold. Chill until firm. Unmold on cold platter garnished with lettuce. Decorate with parsley and lemon peel if desired.

This is an excellent hors d' oeuvre to serve before any type of meal as a cracker spread. It may also be used as a salad.

Liver Paté

1   **lb. chicken livers**
1   **bay leaf**
3   **stalks celery, sliced**
1   **cube soft butter**
3   **ozs. brandy**
1   **tablespoon dry mustard**
    salt, onion salt, pepper to taste

Boil livers in salted water with bay leaf and celery. Drain well; then chop livers and cream with butter, brandy, and mustard. Add seasonings to taste. Spread on crackers for an excellent hors d' oeuvre.

Liverwurst Mold

1   **package unflavored gelatine**
¼   **cup cold water**
1   **10½ oz. can beef consommé**
1   **small bottle green olives,**
    stuffed with pimientos
1½   **3 oz. packages cream cheese**
¾   **lb. liverwurst**
2   **green onions, chopped fine**

Soak gelatine in water. Heat consommé to boiling and add gelatine. Place ½ cup consommé in small ring mold and let congeal, but not until hard. Add sliced olives on top. In separate mixing bowl, cream the cheese, liverwurst, onions, and remaining consommé. Pour into the mold. When ready to serve, unmold and serve with rye bread, sliced French bread, or crackers.

Soups

Suggestions

1. Homemade soups seem to have gone out of style because so many people will not take time to do the job. But they really aren't that complicated or time-consuming.

2. I like to serve a soup course instead of a salad occasionally for luncheons or dinners.

3. A thick soup, such as minestrone, can be served as the main course for lunch.

4. Soup can be made one day and served the next. It is always more tasty when re-heated.

5. Many times I make large quantities of soup which I freeze in quart jars or milk cartons. This saves a great amount of work and provides quick, easy meals.

6. To easily remove fat from soups, place several ice cubes in a cloth, tie ends together, and skim surface of soup.

7. Always heat soup plates or cups and serve HOT.

Beef-Pearl Barley Soup

1	2 lb. chuck roast or 3 beef shanks
1	gallon boiling water
1	can solid pack tomatoes, chopped or 3 fresh peeled tomatoes, chopped
½	cup pearl barley
2-3	teaspoons salt
1	teaspoon garlic salt
½	teaspoon pepper
1	small red chili pepper (optional)
2	cloves garlic, chopped fine (optional)
2	zucchini, unpeeled and chopped
1	teaspoon chopped basil
3	tablespoons chopped parsley
½	cup Sebastiani Chardonnay or August Sebastiani Country Fumé Blanc
	grated Parmesan cheese

Trim all fat from meat and put into boiling water. Add tomatoes and barley. If using fresh tomatoes, add ½ teaspoon sugar. Add remaining ingredients and simmer at least 2½ hours. Taste soup when it has cooked 1½ hours—you may want to add more salt. When meat is tender, remove from pot and slice into strips. Serve as an accompaniment to soup with ketchup and mustard. Sprinkle cheese over soup before serving.

When fresh vegetables are in season, add 6 string beans, chopped and ½ cup peas. Carrots can be added to the soup, also, but my husband always said they made the soup too sweet. This soup will taste better heated over the next day and it can also be frozen as this recipe makes a great quantity.

Butter Ball Soup

1½	loaves stale white bread, sliced
1	cube soft butter
3	eggs
	salt, white pepper to taste
4-6	cups chicken broth
2	teaspoons chopped parsley
½	cup uncooked rice (optional)

Remove crusts from bread slices and crumble insides between hands. Add butter and eggs. Mix well and knead until mixture can be formed into small balls. Form balls ¾ inch in diameter and drop into boiling chicken broth. Sprinkle with parsley and add rice, if desired. Cook until rice is tender and serve. Serves 4-6.

This recipe yields quite a large amount of butter ball mixture. Use as much as you desire, then chill or freeze the rest for use on another day.

Chicken Feet Soup

10 chicken feet
6 chicken wings
2 quarts water
2 teaspoons salt
2 stalks celery
1 onion
1 clove garlic
    salt, pepper to taste
¼-½ cup pastina (fine paste)
    cooked according to directions
    on package

Scald chicken feet in salted boiling water, then remove skins and nails. Return to 2 qts. fresh boiling water and add wings, vegetables, and garlic. Let boil an additional 1-2 hours. Then strain and season to taste with salt and pepper. Serve soup with a fine pastina and place chicken parts on a separate platter to serve.

If available, chicken necks may also be added to the soup. Add to boiling water along with chicken wings and vegetables.

Chicken Soup

1 boiling chicken
3 quarts boiling water
2 celery stalks
1 clove garlic
1 onion, whole
2 sprigs parsley
    salt, white pepper to taste
2-3 coils capellini
    grated Parmesan cheese

Place chicken into deep kettle of boiling water along with celery, onion, garlic, salt and pepper. Skim surface occasionally to remove grease while cooking over medium low heat for 2-2½ hours. Remove chicken and cut into pieces. Strain broth and add capellini. Cook 5-10 minutes longer and sprinkle with cheese before serving. Makes about 1½ quarts.

A tradition in our family is to serve this when anyone isn't feeling well as it is very easily digested. Be sure to use only very fine pastina for this recipe and if desired, a few egg yolks may also be dropped into the broth.

Clam Chowder

1   onion, sliced or chopped
2   tablespoons butter
3-4 slices bacon, cut into pieces
1   teaspoon salt
⅛   teaspoon pepper
1   quart minced clams, saving liquid
4   cups diced potatoes
4   cups milk

Sauté onion with butter and bacon. Add salt and pepper. Add cubed potatoes, clam liquor, and water enough to cover. Cook until nearly tender. Add milk and boil; when potatoes are cooked, add clams and cook only 3 minutes longer.

If you prefer tomato clam chowder, substitute tomato sauce for the milk called for in the recipe.

Crab or Shrimp Soup

3   tablespoons butter
3   tablespoons flour
3   cups milk
¼   teaspoon garlic salt
½   teaspoon salt
¼   teaspoon white pepper
8-10 ozs. shrimp or crab (more if
      you like)
1   teaspoon chopped parsley

In top of double boiler, melt butter and add flour. Add milk gradually and cook until thick. Add garlic salt, salt and pepper. Cover and keep on low heat. Just before serving, add fish and parsley. Serves 4.

Egg Soup

4   eggs
2   tablespoons fine semolina
3   scant tablespoons parmesan cheese;
      grated
1   cup cold chicken broth
2½   quarts rich chicken broth
      salt, pepper to taste

Beat eggs, semolina, and parmesan well. Slowly blend in cold chicken broth, beating continuously with a whisk until smooth and without lumps. Bring rich chicken broth to a boil and pour egg mixture all at once into the boiling broth. Reduce heat to a simmer and stir vigorously for 3-4 minutes until slightly flaky. Season with salt and pepper.

Meatball Soup

Meatball ingredients:

½   lb. ground beef
¼   cup uncooked oatmeal
½   small onion, chopped fine
1   clove garlic, pressed
2   tablespoons grated Parmesan cheese
1   teaspoon chopped parsley
¼   teaspoon garlic salt
½   teaspoon salt
⅛   teaspoon pepper
2   tablespoons tomato sauce
1½   teaspoons August Sebastiani Country Cabernet Sauvignon or Country Zinfandel
1   egg, beaten

Broth:

2   quarts boiling water
2   teaspoons salt
1   teaspoon garlic salt
2   stalks tender celery, chopped fine
2   teaspoons chopped parsley
1   small onion, chopped
1   teaspoon chopped basil (optional)
2   celery leaves, chopped (optional)
4   tablespoons tomato sauce
½   cup uncooked rice
     grated Parmesan cheese

Combine all meatball ingredients together and mix well. Form into small balls. Add seasonings, all vegetables, and tomato sauce to boiling water. Then add meatballs. Let simmer 45 minutes. Add rice and let simmer another 20 minutes. Sprinkle with cheese before serving. Makes 3 quarts.

You may add any other vegetables of your choice to this soup. Salt and pepper to suit your individual taste.

Rice-Milk Soup

4   cups milk
½   cup uncooked rice
1   teaspoon salt

In top of a double boiler, bring milk to just under boiling. Add rice and salt and stir frequently. Cook, covered, 30 minutes, and stir occasionally until rice is tender. Serves 4.

Quick Minestrone

1	11 oz. can red kidney beans
1	teaspoon salt
½	teaspoon garlic salt
1	clove garlic, pressed
¼	teaspoon pepper
1	tablespoon oil
¼	cup chopped parsley
1	small zucchini, unpeeled and cut into small cubes
2	stalks celery, chopped
1	small carrot, diced
2	green onions, chopped
4-5	leaves Swiss chard, chopped
3	tablespoons butter
1	8 oz. can tomato sauce or 1 can solid pack tomatoes, mashed
2½	cups water
½	cup Sebastiani "Eye of the Swan" Pinot Noir Blanc or Chenin Blanc
¼	cup uncooked elbow macaroni (optional) grated Parmesan cheese

Place undrained beans in a large kettle or saucepan; mash about ⅔ of the beans and leave the rest whole. Add salt, garlic salt, garlic, pepper, oil and parsley, stirring well. Then add all the vegetables, butter, tomato sauce and water. Simmer 1 hour or more and then add sherry. (If desired, macaroni may be added at this point.) Simmer 10-15 minutes longer. Sprinkle with cheese before serving. Serves 6. If soup seems too thick add more water and salt to taste.

Minestrone is an old recipe that used to take about half a day to prepare, starting with dry red beans. This is a modern version using canned kidney beans and it is equally as good as the old. I usually serve it with garlic bread and a salad and this makes a very nourishing meal. If available, several leaves of fresh basil, chopped fine, will give added flavor. Sometimes, I also add ½ cup grated or cubed potatoes. The longer minestrone is cooked, the better will be the flavor.

Ravioli or Tortellini in Broth

4	cups canned chicken broth
24	ravioli or tortellini
2	teaspoons chopped parsley grated Parmesan cheese

Bring chicken broth to boil and add ravioli or tortellini. Cook until tender, about 15 minutes. Sprinkle with parsley and grated cheese before serving.

This soup makes a fine first course for dinner. It's soup and pasta all in one!

Split Pea Soup

1½   cups split peas
     ham bone
½   onion, finely chopped
1   cup celery, finely chopped
6   cups boiling water
1   clove garlic, chopped
     dash of cayenne
2   tablespoons butter
2   tablespoons flour
     salt to taste
     paprika

Add peas, ham bone, onion, and celery to boiling water. Then add garlic and cayenne. Simmer, covered, for 2 hours. Put the soup through a sieve. Chill and remove grease. Melt butter and stir in flour until well-blended. Add a little of the soup mixture slowly. Cook and stir until it boils then add to the rest of the soup. Season soup with salt and paprika. Serves 6.

Oyster Soup

2   tablespoons butter
1   cup finely chopped celery
2   tablespoons flour
1   pint milk
1   pint stewing oysters
2   teaspoons chopped parsley
4   teaspoons Sebastiani "Eye of the Swan" Pinot Noir Blanc or Chenin Blanc
     salt, paprika to taste

Simmer butter and celery in top of double boiler until tender. Blend in flour. Add milk and seasoning, stirring well. Clean oysters and chop fine. When ready to serve soup, add oysters, parsley, and wine to taste. Heat thoroughly, but do not cook. Serves 4.

Farinata

3½   cups chicken broth
1   clove garlic, pressed
2   teaspoons chopped parsley
2   tablespoons polenta
4   leaves escarole, cut into 1 inch strips (romaine lettuce or kale may be used instead)

Bring broth to boil. Add garlic, parsley, and polenta. Let simmer, covered for 40 minutes. Add lettuce and cook 10 minutes longer. Serves 4.

This is a truly different and delicious soup. If kale is used, cook 10 minutes longer.

Pasta & Rice

Suggestions

1. When boiling pasta, add one teaspoon salt for every four cups of water. Also, if one tablespoon of oil is added to the boiling water, the pasta will not stick together.

2. A tablespoon of vinegar added to homemade noodles will keep them from being tough.

3. A few drops of lemon juice added to rice while it is boiling will keep the grains separated and make the rice whiter.

Baked Lasagna

1   12 oz. package lasagna noodles
1   lb. ricotta cheese (optional)
½   lb. mozzarella cheese, sliced thin
½   lb. grated swiss cheese
     salt, pepper to taste
     spaghetti sauce (see recipe in this section)
     grated Parmesan cheese

Cook lasagna noodles in boiling salted water, adding a few drops of olive oil to the water. Cook as directed on package and drain immediately. Immerse noodles in cold water. In a greased shallow casserole, arrange a layer of lasagna. Spread a layer of ricotta over this, then a layer of spaghetti sauce, then a layer of mozzarella, topping all with a sprinkling of swiss cheese. Repeat layers in this order until all ingredients are used, ending with a layer of sauce and a sprinkling of grated Parmesan. Bake at 350 degrees for 50 minutes. Remove from oven and let stand about 15 minutes so that it will be easy to cut. Serves 8.

I have made ricotta cheese optional in this recipe as I have found that the lasagna is good even without it.

Canelloni

1   8 oz. package canelloni
     spaghetti sauce (see recipe in this section)

Meat filling:
4   tablespoons olive oil
1   medium onion, chopped
1½   lbs. ground beef
2   tablespoons chopped parsley
     salt, pepper to taste
2   eggs, slightly beaten
¼   lb. mozzarella cheese, diced
¼   lb. swiss cheese, grated
1   cup bread crumbs
⅔   cup milk

Place up to 8 canelloni in 6 qts. boiling water. Cook for 5 minutes only. Remove carefully with strainer spoon. Run cold water over shells until cool enough to handle. Make meat filling by first sautéing onion in oil. Add ground meat and season while meat cooks. When well-browned remove from heat and let cool. Mix in eggs, cheeses, bread crumbs, and milk. Fill canelloni, using a butter knife; then refrigerate until ready to use. When ready to bake, cover bottom of a baking dish with spaghetti sauce. Lay canelloni in side by side and cover with sauce. Cover dish with aluminum foil, crimping edges to seal. Bake in 400 degree oven for 40 minutes. Remove foil and bake another 10 minutes. Serves 8.

When I have a small fresh Italian sausage on hand, I break it into very small pieces and mix it with the beef prior to browning. It adds to the flavor of the filling considerably.

Malfatti

2   packages frozen spinach
½   loaf dry French bread
1   medium onion, chopped fine
1   clove garlic, chopped
1-2   cups dry bread crumbs
1   cup grated Parmesan cheese
½   cup parsley, chopped fine
1   teaspoon salt
¼   teaspoon pepper
1   teaspoon basil, chopped fine
3-4   eggs
      spaghetti sauce (see recipe in this section)
      grated Parmesan cheese

Cook frozen spinach in frying pan with a little water. Squeeze dry and chop fine. Soak bread in hot water and squeeze dry. Sauté onion and garlic lightly, seasoning with salt and pepper. Mix together spinach, bread, onion, and garlic. (If possible, use a meat grinder for this process.) Mix in bread crumbs, cheese, parsley, and basil. Break in eggs and mix well. Season to taste. Take small amount of mixture into floured hands and roll into links like pork sausage. Drop into boiling salted water. When malfattis float to the surface, they are done. Remove a few at a time gently, let drain, and serve with spaghetti sauce and grated cheese. Serves 12.

Malfatti are for the adventurous cook since they are a bit tricky. If desired, malfatti can be prepared the day before and arranged in a baking dish with spaghetti sauce poured over all. Simply refrigerate overnight and heat before serving in a slow oven until heated thoroughly.

Mock Ravioli

1   lb. ground round
1   onion, chopped
1   clove garlic
1   tablespoon olive oil
1   small can tomato sauce
1½   cups water
1   teaspoon mixed Italian herbs
1   teaspoon fresh thyme
½   cup dry Italian mushrooms
½   lb. butterfly macaroni
      salt, pepper to taste

Spinach Mixture
1½   cups cooked frozen spinach, chopped
½   cup bread crumbs
½   cup chopped parsley
½   cup grated Parmesan cheese
1   clove garlic, chopped
¼   cup olive oil
1   teaspoon salt
1   teaspoon sage
4   eggs, well-beaten

Brown meat, onion, and garlic in oil, adding garlic last. Season with salt and pepper, then add tomato sauce, water, herbs, thyme, and mushrooms. Let simmer 10 minutes. Cook butterfly macaroni in salted boiling water as indicated on package. Prepare spinach mixture by combining all ingredients together and mixing well, making sure that spinach is drained thoroughly before using. Grease a deep, large (8x10) casserole dish. Put a layer of macaroni at bottom of casserole, then spread a layer of spinach mixture over this. Top with a layer of meat mixture. Continue in this manner until dish is full, topping with macaroni and meat sauce. Bake at 350 degrees for 40 minutes. Serves 10-12. If desired, half of this may be frozen for another meal.

Clams with Pasta

1   cube butter
2   cloves garlic, chopped
½   cup Sebastiani Chardonnay
1   7½ oz. can minced clams with their liquid
1   12 oz. package large pasta shells
2   tablespoons chopped parsley
    salt, pepper to taste

This clam sauce is also excellent over boiled rice.

Melt butter in heavy skillet, stir in garlic, and cook over medium heat for a few minutes. Do not let garlic brown. Add wine and clam liquid and simmer 5-6 minutes. Remove from heat and set aside. Boil pasta shells as indicated on package and drain well. Transfer to a heated serving dish. Return sauce to heat and bring to a boil over high heat. Add clams and cook until clams are thoroughly heated. Pour over shells, sprinkle over parsley, and toss together until all ingredients are well-mixed. Season to taste with salt and pepper. Serves 4.

Dough for Egg Pasta

4   cups flour
3   eggs, slightly beaten
2   teaspoons salt
2   tablespoons olive oil
¼-½ cup lukewarm water

Sift flour onto a large pastry board. Make a well in the center and put in slightly-beaten eggs. Add salt and oil and mix flour into eggs, a little at a time. Add water a few drops at a time just enough to make the dough soft enough to knead. Knead dough on floured board with the heel of the hand for 10-12 minutes until it is smooth and elastic. Roll out and cut into desired shapes and sizes for use in recipe of your choice, flour gently, and let dry for at least 1 hour before cooking. May be used for any dish calling for pasta, e.g., spaghetti, lasagna, fettucine.

Fettucine

1   cube soft butter
¼   cup heavy cream
½   cup grated Parmesan cheese
6-8 quarts water
1   tablespoon salt
1   lb. cooked fettucine
    salt, pepper to taste

Cream butter until light and fluffy. Beat in cream a little at a time, then add cheese by tablespoon, beating well after each addition. Cook fettucine in salted boiling water as indicated on package. Drain immediately and thoroughly. Transfer at once to a hot serving bowl. Add butter-cheese mixture to fettucine and toss until all fettucine is well-coated. Taste and season with salt and pepper. Serve at once with additional cheese. Serves about 6.

Pasta con Pesto

Pesto
2	cups fresh basil leaves, coarsely chopped
1-2	sprigs parsley
1	teaspoon salt
½	teaspoon pepper
2	cloves garlic
1	cup olive oil
½	cup grated Parmesan cheese

Pasta
6	ozs. spaghetti rings or your favorite pasta
	salted boiling water
1	medium potato, peeled and cut, or small new potatoes, if available
1	small zucchini, cut into ½ in. rounds or a few cut-up Italian beans (when in season)
2	tablespoons olive oil

Combine basil, parsley, salt, pepper, garlic, and oil in blender. Blend just a few seconds. Stop blender and push herbs down with a rubber spatula. Blend a few seconds, then stop again to push herbs down. Repeat procedure until sauce is fairly thin, but not liquified. Transfer sauce to a bowl and add cheese. Boil pasta, potatoes, and zucchini in water, but not too vigorously. Add 2 tablespoons olive oil, then drain thoroughly, reserving 1 cup of this liquid. Add a little liquid to pesto and pour 4-5 tablespoons pesto over pasta and toss until all pasta is well-coated. The remaining pesto may be refrigerated or frozen for future use. Serves 4.

Pasta for Green Noodles

½	lb. spinach
4	cups flour
2	teaspoons salt
2	tablespoons olive oil
2	eggs, well-beaten
	spaghetti sauce (see recipe in this section)

Cook spinach, drain well, and put through a fine-meshed sieve. Sift flour and salt onto a large pastry board. Make a well in the center and put in oil, eggs, and spinach. Using the fingers, mix well until all ingredients are blended. If necessary, add a few drops of water so that all flour is mixed in. If pasta becomes too soft, add more flour. Knead thoroughly for at least 12 minutes until pasta is smooth and elastic. Divide dough into fourths and roll out each fourth 1/16 inch thich. Roll up each sheet, cut cross-wise into strips of desired width. Let dry for 30 minutes. Use with spaghetti sauce. Serves 8-10.

Potato Gnocchi (Lombard Style)

6	large potatoes, hot and cooked
4	tablespoons butter
3	eggs, slightly beaten
2	teaspoons baking powder
4	cups flour
½	cube melted butter
½	cup grated Parmesan cheese
	salt, white pepper to taste

Mash potatoes. Beat in butter, eggs, and baking powder. Salt and pepper to taste. Sift in flour, making a stiff dough. Mix and knead until dough is smooth. Shape dough into long rolls about as thick as a finger and cut into 1 inch pieces. Pressing with thumb, roll each gnocchi over the back of a fork. (An easier method is to press each piece with your thumb to make a crescent shape.) Cook gnocchi a few at a time in a large pot of boiling salted water until they rise to the surface about 10 minutes. Remove gently and repeat until all gnocchi are cooked. Arrange in a heated baking dish and sprinkle generously with melted butter and cheese. Set the dish in a 350 degree oven for a few minutes until cheese melts. Serves 6-8.

For people who like the flavor of garlic, follow the above directions, except mince two cloves garlic and add to the melted butter, browning lightly. Pour over cooked gnocchi and add cheese. Spaghetti sauce (see recipe in this section) may also be used as an accompaniment to gnocchi. Simply pour over the gnocchi in the baking dish and let bake a few minutes. Serve with cheese.

Pizza Bread Dough

1	package fresh yeast
2	tablespoons lukewarm water
1	cup boiling water
1½	teaspoons salt
2	tablespoons butter
3	cups sifted flour

Crumble yeast in water for 5 minutes. Pour boiling water over salt and butter, let cool to lukewarm, then add yeast. Add half of flour and beat smooth. Then add remaining flour and beat smooth again. Divide dough in half for this pizza. Use all of dough for thicker pizza. Place dough on floured board and pat gently into 1 13-inch round or 2 11-inch rounds, with edges slightly thicker. Place on greased cookie sheet. Let rise in warm place (85 degrees) until dough doubles in height. Arrange filling on top and bake as directed in pizza filling.

29

Pizza Filling

3   tablespoons olive oil
½   cup grated Parmesan cheese
¾   lb. sliced mozzarella cheese
2   cups diced canned tomatoes,
     peeled and drained
1   clove garlic, minced
½   teaspoon salt
⅛   teaspoon pepper
½   teaspoon dried oregano or thyme

Prepare pizza dough. After dough rises, brush with 1 tablespoon oil. Sprinkle with Parmesan; arrange ⅓ mozzarella on top. Sprinkle with tomatoes mixed with garlic, salt, and pepper. Arrange remaining mozzarella on top. Sprinkle with oregano, then sprinkle on 2 tablespoons oil. Bake in 450 degree oven 25-30 minutes until crust is golden brown.

There are many variations for pizza. Here are just a few:

Anchovy Pizza: Make pizza as above and dot with a 2 oz. can anchovy filets, finely minced. Drizzle on oil from anchovies and garnish with a few slices of green pepper. Bake as directed.

Mushroom Pizza: Make basic pizza. Sprinkle on top ¼ lb. chopped mushrooms, sautéed in 2 tablespoons olive oil with ¼ teaspoon salt for 5 minutes. Bake as directed.

Sausage Pizza: Make basic pizza. Dot surface with thin slices of one Italian sausage from which the skin has been removed. Bake as directed.

To prevent tearing pizza, cut with kitchen shears.

Polenta Casserole

3   quarts water (reduce water if
     thicker polenta is desired)
1½   tablespoons salt
3   cups Polenta
½   cube butter
     spaghetti sauce (see recipe in this
     section)
     grated Parmesan cheese
1   lb. teleme cheese, shredded (optional)

Bring water to a boil; add salt. Measure Polenta into a bowl and add gradually into water. Stir constantly. Turn heat down and continue stirring frequently for 50 minutes. Butter a shallow casserole dish and spread half the polenta in bottom. Put spaghetti sauce and cheese over this, then spread another layer of polenta, again topping with sauce and cheese. Slices of teleme cheese can be used between the layers if desired. Bake in 375 degree oven for 30 minutes. Serves 6-8.

Polenta, a terribly-neglected dish, is very delicious and has many variations. It can be served with Venison Stew, Beef Stew, Pheasant Cacciatore, Chicken Cacciatore, or boiled Italian sausage (see recipes in this book). Simply cook polenta and serve with the stews or cacciatores poured over same on individual plates. For those who like cheese, sprinkle with grated Parmesan. I have learned to cook polenta in a pressure cooker and it works very well. Using 1 cup less water and only 1 tablespoon salt, cook according to pressure cooker directions for 20 minutes. If any polenta is left over, we put the polenta in a bowl

(Polenta Casserole Continued)

and refrigerate. The next day it can be sliced approximately ½ inch thick and fried in oil and butter mixed with a touch of garlic salt.Cook until crusty and serve. Another way to use leftover polenta is to slice it as above and put slices in a buttered shallow baking dish. Top with thin slices of Monterey cheese and bake in a slow oven until cheese melts. Serve immediately.

Noni Pini's Ravioli

Dough:

4	cups flour
1	egg
2	**tablespoons** olive oil
2	teaspoons salt
1	cup warm water

Filling:

1	chicken breast
1½	lbs. ground round or veal
1	set beef brains
3	**tablespoons** butter
2	cloves garlic, chopped fine
1½	bunches spinach
¼	cup chopped parsley
½	cup grated Parmesan cheese
¼	cup swiss cheese, grated
	salt, pepper to taste
3	eggs, slightly beaten

Mix all dough ingredients together and knead for about 20 minutes. Test by pressing finger into dough; when it bounces back, it is ready. Let dough stand about 10 minutes in a covered bowl to rise. Divide dough in half. Roll out one half into a round, letting half of this hang over the edge of the board. Roll out the rest of the dough away from you twice. Stretch dough and then roll it twice side to side, keeping it tight under the pin. Reverse dough and roll the other half in the same manner, flouring lightly as you do. Roll until dough is 1/16 inch thick. Repeat procedure for other half of dough. Let dry 1 hour or place on cookie sheets and freeze overnight. (This makes dough easier to work with).

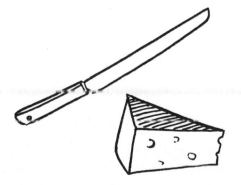

Dice chicken, ground round, and brains. Melt butter in skillet; add meats, sauté lightly. Then add garlic. Salt and pepper to taste. Sauté until meat is tender, then chop fine. Wash spinach thoroughly and cook for 5 minutes. Drain well and chop fine. Add salt and pepper to taste. Combine chopped meats, spinach, and parsley with cheeses and eggs. Makes about 4 cups of filling, enough for 250 small raviolis.

Preparing ravioli:

Take 1 layer of dough and spread half of meat mixture over one half of the dough's surface. Fold other half over and roll with a ravioli rolling pin. Then cut with a ravioli cutter. Repeat process with remaining dough and meat mixture. Boil raviolis in salted boiling water 10-15 minutes until tender when pricked with a fork. Raviolis can be kept frozen up to 4 weeks.

Rice Curry Casserole

3   cups cooked rice
1   can celery soup, undiluted
2   6½ oz. cans tuna
1   teaspoon curry powder
½   cup chopped olives
1   tablespoon grated onion
½   tablespoon salt
1   cup buttered bread crumbs

Combine all ingredients, mixing well. Place in baking dish and bake 25-30 minutes at 375 degrees. Serves 8-10.

Risotto with Mushrooms

½   cup butter
1   medium size onion, minced
1½   cups raw rice
1   small can sliced mushrooms, drained
⅛   teaspoon powdered saffron (optional)
½   cup Sebastiani Chardonnay
4-5 cups boiling chicken broth
½   cup grated Parmesan cheese
½   cup shredded swiss cheese
     salt, white pepper to taste

Melt butter in a large, heavy skillet. Add onions and sauté very slowly, stirring frequently. Do not let them brown. Add rice, then mushrooms and stir gently for a minute or two. Add salt and pepper to taste and stir frequently for about 10 minutes. Dissolve saffron in a tablespoon of heated wine, then add to rice with remaining wine. Add chicken broth a little at a time, stirring for about 25 minutes until rice is tender and all the liquid is absorbed. Stir in cheeses just before serving. Serves 6.

Rice Torte

7   eggs, slightly beaten
2   cups cooked rice
2   medium zucchini, shredded
½   cup olive oil
1   cup grated Parmesan cheese
½   cup chopped parsley
2   green onions, chopped
     salt, pepper to taste

Beat eggs until frothy. Add rice (cooked according to directions on package), zucchini, oil, cheese, parsley, and onions. Season to taste and bake in a casserole dish at 350 degrees for 35-40 minutes or until set.

As a variation of this torte, you can add chopped green peppers instead of the zucchini.

Spaghetti Sauce

1	lb. ground beef (optional)
4	tablespoons olive oil
4	tablespoons butter
4	stalks celery, chopped
4	onions, chopped
4	cloves garlic, chopped fine
¼	teaspoon thyme
¼	teaspoon rosemary
½	cup parsley, chopped fine
½	cup dried Italian mushrooms, soaked in 1 cup hot water and then chopped
1	large can solid pack tomatoes, mashed with liquid
6	8 oz. cans tomato sauce
1½	cups water
1	cup August Sebastiani Chablis or Country Fumé Blanc
1	teaspoon sugar
	salt, pepper to taste

If using meat, brown meat in olive oil and butter. Add celery and onions until brown, then add garlic. Salt and pepper to taste; then add spices, mushrooms with their liquid, tomatoes, and tomato sauce. Rinse tomato sauce cans with water and add to sauce along with wine and sugar. Cook for 3 hours over low heat, stirring occasionally. If not using meat, start by browning onions and celery and proceed as above.

Instead of ground beef, a piece of pot roast can be used. Brown on all sides and proceed as above, letting meat simmer in sauce. After 2 hours, remove meat from sauce and keep warm. Slice and serve as meat course for your dinner. If your family likes their sauce hot, add a small chili pepper, chopped very fine, while sauce is simmering. These peppers are very hot and go a long way, so use them with caution. This recipe yields a quantity of sauce greater than you would normally use at one time. Freeze the remainder in pint jars, filling ¾ full. I always keep a supply of frozen sauce on hand—it helps put together numerous meals in short time.

Spinach Dumplings

2   10 oz. packages frozen chopped spinach
    or 1½ lbs. fresh spinach
4   tablespoons butter
2   teaspoons grated onion
¾   cup ricotta cheese
1   egg, slightly-beaten
6   tablespoons flour
¾   cup grated Parmesan cheese
    salt, pepper to taste
6   quarts water
1   tablespoon salt
    Bisquick
    spaghetti sauce (see recipe in this section)
    grated Parmesan cheese

Cook spinach thoroughly, seasoning with salt and pepper to taste. Squeeze dry and chop fine. Melt butter in skillet over moderate heat and add spinach and onion, stirring constantly 2-3 minutes until most of the moisture is absorbed. Add ricotta cheese, cook 3-4 minutes longer, mixing well. Then remove from heat and let cool. Place cooled spinach mixture in mixing bowl and add egg, flour, cheese, and salt and pepper to taste. Mix all ingredients well, then refrigerate 45 minutes until mixture becomes quite firm. Bring water and salt to a rapid boil. Shape spinach mixture into balls and roll in Bisquick. Drop into boiling water, cooking uncovered 6-7 minutes until they are firm. Gently remove from water and let drain. Arrange dumplings on a platter, pour over spaghetti sauce and sprinkle with cheese. Serves 4-6.

Another way to serve these spinach dumplings is to dribble 4 tablespoons melted butter over them and sprinkle generously with grated Parmesan cheese. Set under broiler until cheese melts and serve with garlic bread for a complete meal.

Rice Casserole

1   tablespoon oil
1   tablespoon butter
1   onion, chopped
1   clove garlic, pressed or
    chopped fine
1   can solid pack tomatoes, mashed
1   cup raw rice
½   cup August Sebastiani Chablis
    or Country Chenin Blanc
1-2 cups leftover meat, cubed-any
    kind will do
    grated Parmesan cheese
    salt, pepper to taste

Brown onion in oil and butter, adding a little salt and pepper. Add garlic and sauté briefly. Then add tomatoes, rice, wine, and meat. Salt and pepper to taste. Cover and bake 40 minutes in 350 degree oven. Sprinkle with cheese just before serving. Serves 4.

Wild Rice

6 tablespoons butter
½ cup chopped parsley
½ cup green onions, chopped
1 cup sliced celery
1½ cups washed wild rice
1 10½ oz. can condensed consommé
1½ cups boiling water
1 teaspoon salt
½ teaspoon marjoram or thyme
½ cup Sebastiani "Eye of the Swan" Pinot Noir Blanc

In heavy skillet combine butter, parsley, onions, and celery. Cook until soft, but not browned, about 10 minutes. Add rice, consommé, water, salt, and spice. Cook covered over low heat about 45 minutes. Stir lightly with fork occasionally and add a little hot water if mixture gets too dry. When rice is tender and liquid absorbed, stir in wine. Cook uncovered about 3 minutes longer, until wine is absorbed. Serves 6-8.

If you like a creamy texture, add ½ can undiluted cream of celery soup.

Vegetables

Suggestions

1. When boiling green vegetables, such as string beans, zucchini, artichokes, sprouts, broccoli, and asparagus, bring salted water to a rolling boil. Then add 2–3 teaspoons olive oil and 1 clove garlic to the water before adding vegetables. The oil and garlic will enhance the flavor and texture of the vegetables.

2. When boiling green vegetables, leave uncovered. This will help keep the vegetables green.

3. White vegetables, such as cauliflower, onions, and turnips, will stay white if pan is left covered while vegetables are boiling and a little lemon juice or vinegar is added to the water.

4. Do not overcook vegetables; they should be firm, not mushy.

5. Just before draining boiled green vegetables, add 1 cup cold water and drain immediately. This will add greenness to the vegetables.

Artichoke Frittata

4   links pork sausage, skinned and cut into small pieces
½   onion, chopped
1   clove garlic, chopped
2   packages frozen artichokes or two 14 oz. cans artichokes, drained well and cut into quarters lengthwise
4   eggs, well-beaten
1   teaspoon chopped parsley (optional)
¼   cup grated Parmesan cheese
    salt, pepper to taste

Sauté sausage with onion and garlic. Add artichokes and cook over low heat until tender, about 10 minutes. Season to taste with salt and pepper. Stir in eggs and turn into an oiled 8x8 baking dish. Sprinkle with parsley and cheese and bake at 350 degrees for 30 minutes. Serves 6.

For variations, this frittata recipe can be used with cooked asparagus, zucchini, and string beans. Simply substitute for the artichokes as indicated above. Sometimes, I make the frittata without cheese.

Stuffed Artichokes

4   artichokes
½   cup vinegar
4   tablespoons olive oil
1½   cups bread crumbs
4   cloves garlic, chopped fine
4   tablespoons grated Parmesan cheese
½   teaspoon salt
1   tablespoon chopped parsley
    pepper to taste

Wash artichokes in water and vinegar to prevent discoloring. Trim bases so that artichokes can stand upright. Trim about ½ inch off points of remaining leaves. Drop artichokes into a large pot of boiling water and boil for 10 minutes. Drain and cool upside down. Then gently spread out top leaves of each artichoke and pull the tender center of thistle-like yellow leaves. Scrape out the hairy choke inside to leave the heart clean. Heat 4 tablespoons oil in a heavy skillet. Add bread crumbs, garlic, cheese, salt, parsley, and pepper. Stir well. Spoon about 2 tablespoonfuls of this stuffing into the center of each artichoke. With fingers, press rest of stuffing between the large outer leaves. Arrange artichokes close together in a deep baking dish and sprinkle 1 tablespoon olive oil over each. Pour in boiling water to a depth of 1 inch. Cover dish tightly and bake for 1 hour at 350 degrees, until tender. Serve immediately. Serves 4.

Artichokes and Peas

2   packages frozen artichokes, unthawed
1   package frozen peas, unthawed
4   tablespoons olive oil
2   tablespoons butter
1   clove garlic, mashed
    salt, pepper to taste

Heat oil and butter in frying pan. Add artichokes and fry slowly. After 15 minutes, add peas. Then add garlic, salt and pepper. Cover for a few minutes and let cook over low heat. Keep turning with pancake turner until artichokes and peas are tender. Remove garlic before serving. Serves 6-8.

Artichokes with Pork Sausage

1 or 2 packages frozen artichokes
4-6   links sausage, cut into 1 in. lengths
    salt, pepper to taste

Cook artichokes and sausage together in frying pan over medium heat for about 20 minutes, seasoning to taste. Keep covered when not stirring. Serves 4-6.

Artichoke Hearts

12   small artichoke hearts, cut in ½,
    or 2 packages frozen hearts
4   tablespoons olive oil
2   tablespoons butter
½   cup Sebastiani "Eye of the Swan" Pinot Noir Blanc or August Sebastiani Country Chardonnay
2   cloves garlic
    salt, pepper to taste

Melt butter with oil in frying pan. Add remaining ingredients and fry together 15-20 minutes. Fresh artichokes will take a couple of minutes longer to cook. Serves 4-6.

Fried Cardone (Wild Artichoke)

1   or 2 stalks cardone, cut into 2 in. pieces
2   cups Bisquick
⅔   cup water
2   eggs
    olive oil
    salt, pepper to taste

Place cardone pieces in boiling salted water for 15-20 minutes, taking care not to overcook. Drain well. Dip cardone into batter made by mixing pancake mix, water, and eggs (mixed thoroughly with a fork). Fry in deep oil and season to taste with salt and pepper.

Boiled Corn

6	ears corn
	cold water
½	cup August Sebastiani Chablis or Country French Colombard

Put ears of corn into large kettle of cold water, making sure all ears are covered with water. Bring to a boil, then add wine. Turn off heat and let stand 20 minutes, or until ready to serve. Serves 6.

Eggplant Italian

1	small eggplant , unpeeled and cubed
1	small dry onion, chopped
6	tablespoons olive oil
1	clove garlic, minced or chopped
	dash minced chili pepper (optional)
½	cup tomato sauce
4	tablespoons grated Parmesan cheese
	salt, pepper to taste

Sauté eggplant and onion in oil, turning frequently with pancake turner. Salt and pepper to taste, then add garlic, and continue cooking until ingredients are tender, about 15-20 minutes. Add chili pepper and tomato sauce and stir occasionally for a few more minutes. Add cheese just prior to serving. Serves 4-6.

Eggplant Parmesan

1½	lbs. eggplant , unpeeled and cut into ½ in. slices
	salt
	flour
¼	cup olive oil
2	cups tomato sauce (see recipes under Miscellaneous)
½	lb. mozzarella or Monterey Jack cheese, sliced thin
½	cup grated Parmesan cheese
2	teaspoons chopped basil

Sprinkle eggplant slices with salt and spread out on a platter. After 30 minutes, pat slices dry with paper towels. Dip each slice into flour and shake off excess. Heat oil in a heavy skillet and brown slices a few at a time. (It may be necessary to add more oil as more eggplant is browned.) After browning, transfer slices to paper towels so that they drain well. Grease well a 2 quart baking dish and pour in ½ cup tomato sauce. Spread eggplant slices over sauce, top with a layer of cheese and a sprinkling of Parmesan and basil. Top with a thin layer of tomato sauce. Repeat layers in this order until all ingredients are used, being sure to finish with a top layer of tomato sauce over the cheeses and basil. Bake for 30 minutes at 350 degrees, or until eggplant is tender when pricked with a fork. Serves 4-6.

Dutch Cabbage

6 tablespoons cider vinegar
6 tablespoons water
4 tablespoons bacon grease
2 tablespoons sugar
6 cups red cabbage, finely shredded
  (about 1 medium head)
  salt, pepper to taste

Put vinegar, water, bacon grease, and sugar in skillet over low heat. Add cabbage, then salt and pepper to taste. Cover and cook slowly over very low heat, stirring occasionally. Serves 4.

Carrots in Wine

1 bunch carrots, sliced
  salted water
3 green onions, chopped
½ clove garlic, pressed
2 tablespoons butter
1 tablespoon flour
¼ cup canned consommé,
  undiluted
½ cup Sebastiani Chardonnay
  salt, pepper to taste

Cover and steam carrots for 15 minutes in a small amount of salted water. Then drain well. In another pan, sauté onion and garlic in melted butter until golden brown. Add flour, then gradually stir in consommé and wine. Cook, stirring constantly, until thick. Add cooked carrots to sauce, then cover and reheat until bubbly. Season to taste with salt and pepper. Serves 6.

Golden Carrot Ring

5 cups grated raw carrots
4 eggs
2 cups half and half cream
1 teaspoon salt
½ teaspoon pepper
1 teaspoon sugar
1 tablespoon lemon juice
1 cup shredded almonds
  butter to grease ring mold

Cook carrots in boiling water, then drain thoroughly. Mix all other ingredients together and combine with carrots. Spread butter thoroughly over inside of 9 inch ring mold. Line with greased wax paper, then pour carrot mixture into mold and bake in 325 degree oven for 40 minutes. Turn onto a large plate and fill center with any other vegetable or mushrooms. Serves 12-14 easily for a buffet.

Carrot Loaf

1 large bunch carrots, cut into small pieces
2 large white onions, chopped
½ lb. very sharp cheddar cheese, shredded
4 eggs, beaten
salt, white pepper to taste

Cook carrots and onions in salted boiling water until carrots are tender. Drain thoroughly and mash. Add cheese and eggs, then salt and pepper to taste. Grease baking mold well, then pour in carrot mixture. Place mold in a shallow baking pan with water. Bake at 325 degrees for 1 hour or more. Mold is ready when it is firm when tested with a knife. Serves 8-10.

Baked Eggplant

1 eggplant, cut into ½″ slices
⅓-½ cup mayonnaise.
⅓ cup saltine crackers, crushed
⅓ cup grated Parmesan cheese

Spread mayonnaise on both sides of egg plant slices. Dip slices into a mixture of cracker crumbs and cheese. Bake on cookie sheet in 400 degree oven for 15-20 minutes or until eggplant is tender.

Fried Mustard Greens

mustard greens
olive oil
1 clove garlic
salt
pepper
kidney beans (optional)

Pick only young tender leaves of mustard green, none of the yellow flowers. Wash well. Put greens in a large pot with just enough water on bottom to keep greens from sticking. Cover and cook until greens are limp. Drain and squeeze dry. Then chop. Put chopped greens into oiled frying pan with whole clove garlic and a few cooked kidney beans and fry until greens are hot.

Once you've developed a taste for these, you'll be out every spring hunting for mustard greens.

Steamed Mustard Greens

mustard greens
olive oil
1 clove garlic
salt
pepper

Place clean greens in oiled pan. Simmer, covered, over low fire and stir occasionally until tender. Serve hot and season to taste.

These greens are somewhat bitter to people who haven't developed a taste for mustard greens.

Peas with Proscuitto
(Italian Ham or Bacon)

2 tablespoons butter
4 tablespoons onion, chopped fine
2 slices bacon cut in 1 in. strips or equivalent amount of prosciutto cut in same manner
1 clove garlic, pressed
¼ cup August Sebastiani Chablis or Country Fumé Blanc
2 10 oz. packages frozen peas
   salt, pepper to taste

Melt butter in skillet and add onions and meat. Cook, stirring frequently, until onions are soft, not brown. Add garlic, then wine. Add peas and let simmer 15 minutes over low fire until peas are tender. Salt and pepper to taste before serving. Serves 4-6.

Green Peppers in Vinegar

5-6 green peppers
1   teaspoon salt
3-4 cloves garlic
1   cup white vinegar
1   cup water
3-4 grape leaves

Wash peppers, remove seeds, and cut into quarters. Pack into a quart jar. Add salt and garlic. Boil together vinegar and water and pour over peppers. Add grape leaves, allowing a little vinegar to cover the leaves. Fill jar to top with vinegar and water and seal immediately. Makes 1 quart.

The addition of grape leaves to the peppers keeps them firm and prevents them from getting mushy.

Stuffed Peppers

4   medium peppers
1   onion chopped
2   tablespoons butter
1   cup cooked rice
1½ cups cooked meat, ground
1   lb. can tomatoes with liquid
    (mashed)
½ cup grated Parmesan cheese
    salt, pepper to taste
½ cup August Sebastiani Country
    Zinfandel or Country
    Cabernet Sauvignon

Cut stem end from peppers and remove seeds and veins. Cook in rapidly boiling salted water, uncovered, for 5 minutes. Remove and turn upside down to drain well. Sauté onion lightly in butter. Add rice, and meat, along with cheese. Season to taste with salt and pepper. Mix well and stuff mixture into peppers. Place in a deep casserole and surround with tomatoes and wine. Bake 45 minutes to 1 hour at 350 degrees, basting peppers occasionally. Spoon tomatoes over peppers before serving. Serves 4.

Baked Potatoes in Foil

potatoes
olive oil
salt
pepper
garlic salt

Rub potatoes with oil, then sprinkle generously with salt, pepper, and garlic salt. Wrap in foil and bake approximately 1 hour in a 350 degree oven. When prepared in this manner, the potato skins are very delicious to eat.

Grated Potatoes

3   medium-sized potatoes
2   tablespoons butter
1   teaspoon olive oil
    salt, pepper to taste

Pare, wash, and grate potatoes on a medium grater. Spread them in a skillet that has been well-greased with oil and butter. Cook potatoes on medium heat, covered, until bottom is brown. Season with salt and pepper. With a pancake turner, reverse and brown the other sides. Season again and serve hot from the pan. Serves 6.

Green Potatoes

6   large potatoes
¾   cup light cream
1   teaspoon sugar
½   cup butter
2   teaspoons salt
¼   teaspoon pepper
1   package frozen chopped spinach,
     cooked and well-drained

Boil potatoes with their skins on. Peel and mash. Add cream, sugar, butter, salt and pepper. Chop spinach fine and add to potato mixture. Beat all together until well-blended. Bake in 400 degree oven for 20-30 minutes until thoroughly heated. Serves 8-10.

This recipe can be prepared ahead and refrigerated until ready to use. Allow 5-10 minutes longer baking time if potatoes are refrigerated before baking.

Potato Slices in Onion Butter

½   cup melted butter
½   package onion soup mix
1   teaspoon salt
½   cup water
4 or 5   medium sized potatoes,
     unpeeled and sliced
     pepper to taste

In mixing bowl, combine butter, soup mix, salt, and pepper. Pour water into a 2 quart casserole. Arrange a layer of potato slices in casserole, then spread a tablespoonful of onion mixture over this. Repeat, making 5 layers. Cover and bake 45 minutes to 1 hour at 350 degrees. Serves 8-10.

Scalloped Potatoes and Onions

4   cups potatoes, pared and sliced thin
1   onion, peeled and sliced thin
3   tablespoons butter
1½   teaspoons salt
     white pepper to taste
3   tablespoons flour
1½   cups milk

Grease a baking dish, preferably with butter. Place potato slices in dish in layers and sprinkle with onion, salt, pepper, and flour. Dot with butter, then pour milk over all. Bake in a 325 degree oven for 1½ hours. A foil cover may be used the first ½ hour if desired. If so, cooking time will be reduced. Serves 6-8.

For an interesting variation, substitute condensed mushroom soup for the flour and milk.

Stuffed Potatoes

5 potatoes
1 cup cottage cheese and chives
1 cube butter
1 egg
2 tablespoons mayonnaise
½ teaspoon Accent
   salt, pepper, garlic salt to taste
   paprika

Bake potatoes until thoroughly cooked. Cut each potato in half and scoop out the insides. Save skins. Using an electric mixer, mix potato insides with cottage cheese, butter, and remaining ingredients. Beat until all ingredients are thoroughly blended, seasoning to taste. Restuff the potato skins with this mixture, sprinkle with paprika, and bake in a 450 degree oven for 15 minutes. Serves 10.

Leftover Mashed Potato Pancakes

1-2 cups cold mashed potatoes
1   or 2 beaten eggs
2   or 3 tablespoons flour
     salt, pepper to taste
3   or 4 tablespoons butter

Add egg, flour, salt and pepper to potatoes and shape into little pancakes. Fry in butter and turn once after browned on one side.

Here is an excellent use for cold mashed potatoes. These are a good compliment to any dinner.

Leftover Potatoes with Tomato Sauce

     leftover mashed potatoes
1   tablespoon chopped parsley
1   clove garlic, chopped
2   tablespoons butter
¼-½ cup tomato sauce

Saute´ garlic and parsley lightly in butter. Add tomato sauce (this amount determined by the amount of potatoes). Add potatoes and stir well with fork over low heat until hot.

Creamed Spinach and Mushrooms

2 tablespoons green onions, chopped
2 tablespoons butter
¼ cup flour
1 teaspoon salt
   dash of pepper
1½ cups light cream
½ cup August Sebastiani Country French Colombard
2 cups cooked spinach, chopped
½ cup cooked mushrooms

Cook onions lightly in butter; stir in flour, salt, and pepper. Slowly stir in cream; cook and stir until mixture boils and thickens. Add wine and cook a few minutes longer. Cook spinach, drain well, and squeeze dry. Add spinach and mushrooms to cream sauce and heat well. Serves 6-8.

Spinach Almondine

2 packages frozen chopped spinach
1 can cream of mushroom soup
2 tablespoons butter
   pinch of ground mace
½ cup blanched and slivered almonds, browned in butter

Thaw and drain spinach well. Place in a casserole and add remaining ingredients. Sprinkle a few almonds on top and cook in a 375 degree oven for 45 minutes. Serves 6-8.

Spinach Loaf

5 tablespoons butter
½ onion, grated
1½ cups milk
5 level tablespoons flour
1 clove garlic, pressed
¼ cup grated Parmesan cheese
½ teaspoon white pepper
½ teaspoon salt
½ cup chopped mushrooms, drained (optional)
3 eggs, separated
2 packages frozen spinach, cooked, drained, and chopped fine

In top of double boiler, melt butter and add onion. Gradually add flour and milk, stirring constantly. Cook until thick, then remove from heat. Beat eggs in a mixing bowl, then gradually stir in onion-milk mixture. Add garlic, cheese, white pepper, salt, and mushrooms. Let cool. Beat egg whites and fold into mixture along with spinach. Turn into a loaf pan or casserole and bake at 350 degrees 30-35 minutes until firm. Serves 4.

This dish can also be baked in a mold. Grease the mold well, then line with wax paper that has also been greased. Pour the mixture into the mold and place mold in a pan. Add enough simmering water to reach about ¾ way up the sides of the mold. Bake in the middle shelf of oven, making sure that temperature is regulated so that water is kept at a very low simmer.

Sherry-Glazed Yams

3 large or 6 medium yams
1 cup Dry Sherry or Cream Sherry
1 teaspoon grated orange rind
½ cup sugar
½ cup brown sugar
4 tablespoons butter

Parboil yams in their jackets. When tender, drain, peel, and cut each yam into 4 or 6 pieces. Place in a buttered shallow baking dish. Combine remaining ingredients. Cook over low heat, stirring constantly, until thick. Pour over yams. Bake uncovered at 350 degrees for 25 minutes. Serves 6.

Asparagus Parmesan

2 lbs. fresh asparagus
6 tablespoons melted butter
½ cup grated Parmesan cheese

Cut off hard ends of asparagus and peel off some of the skin. Cook asparagus in salted boiling water for about 12 minutes. Drain the stalks and place them into a shallow baking dish. Pour over melted butter and sprinkle with parmesan cheese (over the tips). Bake in a 400 degree oven for about 10 minutes.

Swiss Chard

2	bundles Swiss Chard, greens only
2	tablespoons butter
2	tablespoons olive oil
1	clove garlic
	salt, pepper to taste

Boil Swiss chard in salted water until not quite tender. Heat butter and oil in frying pan and add garlic. Add well-drained chard and simmer for 15 minutes. Season to taste with salt and pepper and remove garlic before serving. Serves 4-6.

The white stalks of the Swiss chard can be prepared in this same manner, but they require a longer cooking time. If desired, steam the stalks with butter and sprinkle with Parmesan cheese before serving.

Zucchini and Eggs

4	tablespoons oil
4 or 5	small zucchini cut in pieces
½	onion, chopped
2	eggs
	salt, pepper, garlic salt to taste
	grated Parmesan cheese

Melt butter and oil. Sauté zucchini and onion together, seasoning to taste. Break in eggs and stir, mixing well. As soon as eggs are cooked, remove from heat, top with cheese and serve immediately. Serves 6.

Fried Zucchini

2	tablespoons butter
2	tablespoons olive oil
½	onion, chopped
¼	teaspoon garlic salt
¼	teaspoon salt
⅛	teaspoon pepper
4	medium zucchini, unpeeled and sliced or cubed

Melt butter in oil in frying pan. Add onion and seasonings and sauté until golden brown, stirring frequently. Add zucchini and turn occasionally with pancake turner until tender. Serves 4.

Zucchini Loaf

4 or 5 zucchini, medium size
4   tablespoons chopped green onion
4   tablespoons grated Parmesan cheese
⅓   cup cracker crumbs
4   eggs, beaten
    salt, pepper, garlic salt to taste
⅓   cup chopped parsley (optional)

Cut zucchini into 1 inch rounds and boil for 20 minutes. Drain well, place in saucepan, and mash. Add onions and cheese and seasonings. Add eggs and mix well. Turn onto greased loaf pan and bake at 350 degrees for 30 minutes. Serves 4. This can also be served cold, cut into cubes.

Zucchini Pancakes

2   cups buttermilk pancake mix
⅔   cup water
2   eggs
2   tablespoons grated Parmesan cheese
    salt, pepper to taste
2   large zucchini, unpeeled and shredded
    oil
    butter

Make batter with pancake mix, water, eggs, cheese, and salt and pepper to taste. Put shredded zucchini into batter and mix well. Spoon out with a large spoon and fry in oil and butter at medium heat. Turn when brown. Serves 6-8.

Zucchini Stuffed with Cheese

6   medium size zucchini, whole and unpeeled
8   ozs. sharp Tillamook cheese
    salt, pepper to taste

Cook zucchini in boiling salted water until tender, but firm, about 10-15 minutes. Drain and cut into halves. Remove seeds with a thin knife and sprinkle with salt and pepper. Cut cheese to size necessary to fill the zucchini and bake in a 350 degree oven for 20 minutes. Serves 6-8.

Zucchini Fritters

1-2 zucchini, unpeeled
1 cup cold water
1½ cups Bisquick
1 egg
1 tablespoon grated Parmesan cheese
   salt, pepper, garlic salt to taste
   olive oil

Slice zucchini into long, thin ovals. Add water to pancake mix, beating with a fork. Add egg and continue beating until smooth. Add cheese and seasonings to taste. Dip zucchini into this batter and fry on both sides in deep oil. Sprinkle a little more salt on top and serve at once. Serves 4.

If batter is allowed to stand, it will thicken and it will be necessary to add more water. When in season, zucchini flowers can be prepared in this manner. Be sure to remove the pistil from the flowers first and handle them gently while dipping into the batter as they are fragile. This batter recipe can also be used with any other cooked vegetables, e.g., cauliflower, celery, broccoli, and artichokes. Other variations include adding pre-cooked mushrooms, 1 pressed clove garlic, ½ cup parsley, or 1 small carton sour cream to the batter before using, and reduce the amount of water to ½ cup.

Stuffed Zucchini

4 medium zucchini, unpeeled
2 tablespoons olive oil
1 tablespoon butter
½ cup onions, chopped fine
4 links sausage, chopped fine (optional)
1 clove garlic, pressed
1 egg, lightly beaten
2 ozs. prosciutto, chopped fine (optional)
½ cup fresh bread crumbs
6 tablespoons grated Parmesan cheese
½ teaspoon oregano
   salt, pepper to taste

Boil zucchini about 10 minutes, then cut in half lengthwise and scoop out most of the pulp. Set shells aside and chop pulp. Heat oil and butter in a heavy skillet and cook onions and sausage. Add zucchini pulp and garlic and cook for about 5 minutes, stirring frequently. Pour into a large sieve and let drain. Into this mixture, beat the egg, prosciutto, bread crumbs, 2 teaspoons cheese, oregano, and salt and pepper to taste. Spoon this into hollowed zucchini shells, mounding tops slightly. Place into an oiled shallow baking dish, sprinkle with remaining cheese, and dribble a few drops of olive oil over each shell. Cover dish tightly with foil and bake for 30 minutes at 375 degrees. Remove foil and bake another 10 minutes. Serves 4-6.

Fish

Abalone Trimmings (Dark Trimmings)

2 cups abalone trimmings
4 cups salted boiling water
(using 2 teaspoons salt)
1 tablespoon olive oil
2 tablespoons vinegar
¼ teaspoon sweet basil
1 teaspoon chopped parsley
1 clove garlic, chopped
¼ teaspoon dry mustard
¼ teaspoon pepper
¼ teaspoon oregano
dash or two cayenne pepper

Bring salted water to a rolling boil and add abalone trimmings. Boil about 3 minutes. Drain off 1 cup water from trimmings and set them aside to cool. Add oil, vinegar, spices, and seasonings to remaining water and mix well. Pour over drained and cooled trimmings and pack into jars. Cover and keep in refrigerator for a couple of days.

Arringe (Bloaters or Smoked Herring)

1 arringe
olive oil

Cut fish lengthwise into 1½ inch strips. Fry in olive oil, about 2-3 minutes on each side. Drain well. Just prior to serving, dribble over fresh olive oil.

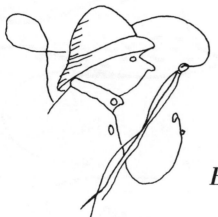

Baccala

1 lb. salted codfish
1 or 2 dried onions, chopped fine
6 tablespoons olive oil
1 tablespoon chopped parsley
¼ teaspoon pepper
1½ tablespoons flour
1¼ cups milk

Soak fish in cold water for 8 hours, changing water several times. Place fish in cold water (enough to cover) and bring to a boil. Drain and place on baking dish. Sauté onions in oil. When soft, add parsley, pepper, and flour and blend well. Pour mixture over fish, then add milk, and stir liquid together. Bake fish at least 1 hour in 275 degree oven. Serves 4.

If desired, this recipe can be prepared with tomato sauce. Substitute one 8 oz. can tomato sauce for the milk and eliminate flour.

Calamari (Squid) *in Tomato Sauce*

2	tablespoons oil
4	tablespoons butter
½	onion, chopped
2	cloves garlic, chopped
1	tablespoon parsley, chopped
1	8 oz. can tomato sauce
¼	cup Sebastiani Sauvignon Blanc or August Sebastiani Country Chardonnay
1	lb. squid, body cut into 1 in. pieces, leaving heads whole
	salt, pepper to taste

Melt butter and oil in frying pan and sauté onions lightly, seasoning to taste with salt and pepper. Add garlic and parsley and sauté for 1 minute. Add tomato sauce and wine. Cover and simmer 15-20 minutes. Then add fish and cook for an additional 12-15 minutes. Take care not to overcook as fish will become tough. Serve at once. Serves 4-6.

Calamari (Squid) *in Wine*

1	lb. squid, body cut into 1 in. pieces, leaving heads whole
2	tablespoons oil
4	tablespoons butter
1	clove garlic, pressed
1	tablespoon parsley, chopped
1	cup Sebastiani Sauvignon Blanc or August Sebastiani Country Chardonnay
	salt, pepper to taste

Lightly brown squid in oil and butter in frying pan, seasoning to taste with salt and pepper. Add garlic and parsley and sauté briefly. Then add wine, stir once, and cover and simmer 12-15 minutes. Serves 4-6.

Cracked Crab

2	cooked crabs
	juice of 6 lemons
	1 or 2 ozs. vinegar
	1 or 2 ozs. olive oil
	dash of paprika
	dash of pepper
	few drops of tabasco sauce
	few drops of Worcestershire sauce

Break off claws from crab and crack with nutcracker. Pull off backs and remove all spongy parts below. Pull off small piece of shell on underside of crab and remove fat. Set aside. Cut body of each crab into 6 pieces. Combine crab fat with remaining ingredients and pour mixture over crab meat and crab legs. Marinate several hours or overnight, turning occasionally. Serve with French bread, large towel bibs, and a Sebastiani dry white wine.

Easy Deviled Crab

3 tablespoons butter or margarine
2 tablespoons flour
1 cup milk, heated
1 teaspoon salt
   dash cayenne pepper
1 teaspoon Worcestershire sauce
2 egg yolks, slightly beaten
2 cups crabmeat, fresh, frozen
   or canned
½ teaspoon lemon juice
¼ cup Sebastiani "Eye of the Swan"
   Pinot Noir Blanc or
   Chardonnay
4 individual baking shells
⅔ cup buttered bread crumbs
4 lemon slices
   paprika

Melt butter; stir in flour and milk. Season with salt, cayenne, and Worcestershire. Cook, stirring constantly, until thick. Add egg yolks and crab while stirring. Cook 3 minutes and stir in lemon juice and wine. Spoon mixture into individual baking shells or ramekins and cover with buttered crumbs. Top with a lemon slice and a sprinkling of paprika. Bake in a 450 degree oven about 20-25 minutes until brown. Serves 4.

Crab or Shrimp Soufflé

4 slices white bread
1 can·crab or shrimp
½ cup mayonnaise
½ cup chopped green onions,
   tops only
½ cup parsley, chopped fine
1 small can water chestnuts, sliced
1 small can mushrooms
2 eggs
1¼ cups milk
½ cup Sebastiani "Eye of the Swan"
   Pinot Noir Blanc or
   Chardonnay
½ cup cream of mushroom soup
½ cup grated Parmesan cheese

Grease a deep casserole. Dice 2 slices of bread and place in bottom. Mix fish, mayonnaise, onions, parsley, water chestnuts, and mushrooms. Spread over bread cubes, then lay 2 slices of bread over this. Beat eggs into milk and wine and pour over entire casserole. Let stand in refrigerator overnight, covered. Bake 20 minutes at 325 degrees. Spread top with mushroom soup and cheese, then bake for an additional hour. Serves 6-8.

When fresh crab is in season, I use a double amount (2 cups) in this recipe.

Cioppino

1   large cooked crab, 2-3 lbs.
½   cup olive oil
½   small white onion, chopped
1   large clove garlic, chopped
2   tablespoons chopped parsley
1   cup August Sebastiani Country
    Chardonnay or Country Fumé Blanc
1   8 oz. can tomato sauce
    dash cayenne pepper
1   tablespoon dry Italian Mushrooms,
    chopped (optional)
¼   teaspoon salt
⅛   teaspoon pepper
1   lb. Ling cod, cut in large chunks
½   lb. frozen or fresh prawns
1½ lbs. clams in shells

Crack crab legs, but leave whole. Crack shell, take out meat, and cut into large chunks. Retain fat from the wings of the shell. Brown onion and garlic in large pot over medium heat. Add parsley and fat of crab. Mix well, then add wine, tomato sauce, seasonings, and mushrooms. Cover and simmer over low heat for 20-30 minutes. Add fish, prawns, and clams. Let cook over low heat for 20 minutes. Do not stir; simply shake the pot occasionally. Add crab and heat just until crab becomes hot. Take care not to stir. Serve immediately. Serves 4-6.

If raw crab is used, add to cioppino along with the other raw fish and cook as usual, keeping crab on the bottom of the pot. There are many variations to this dish: any type of shellfish, e.g., lobster or mussels, can be used. Bass may also be added if you wish. When serving this dish, fingers are the best utensils to use since the crab, prawns, and clams are still in their shells. Each guest would appreciate a dish towel to help him along while he enjoys this dish. We serve a mixed green salad, a Sebastiani dry white wine, and lots of French bread along with cioppino for a complete meal.

Filet of Sole with Grapes

¼   cup butter
1   lb. small filets of sole
½   teaspoon salt
1   tablespoon lemon juice
    sprinkle of cayenne pepper
½   cup August Sebastiani Chablis or
    Country French Colombard
½   cup white seedless grapes, halved
½   teaspoon fresh lemon peel, grated
1   teaspoon chervil

Melt butter in heavy frying pan; add filets and cook for about 5 minutes until slightly browned. Turn carefully with a spatula, sprinkling with salt, lemon juice, and cayenne. Pour wine over fish and continue cooking until done, about 5 minutes. With a spatula, gently lift fish onto heated serving plates or platter. Add grapes, lemon peel, and chervil to the sauce left in the pan. Bring sauce to a boil and simmer until the grapes are heated through. Pour over the filets and serve at once. Serves 4.

Baked Fish

1   3-5 lb. striped bass
1   onion, chopped
4   tablespoons oil
6   tablespoons butter
1   large can solid pack tomatoes,
      mashed, with liquid
2   potatoes, peeled and sliced thin
2-3 teaspoons chopped parsley
2   cloves garlic
¾   cup Sebastiani Chardonnay or
      Sauvignon Blanc
      salt, pepper, garlic salt to taste
1   lemon, sliced thin

Sauté onion in oil and 2 tablespoons butter, adding salt, pepper, and garlic salt to taste. Add tomatoes with their liquid; then add potatoes and cook until potatoes are almost tender. Meanwhile prepare fish. Cut slits across width of fish every 2 in. on both sides and season generously with salt, pepper, and garlic salt. Mix and chop together parsley and garlic, then rub in slits and inside fish. Place in shallow oiled baking dish. Cut 4 tablespoons butter into pieces and place on top of fish. Bake at 350 degrees a few minutes until butter is melted and slightly brown. Pour wine over fish, then pour over the tomato-potato mixture. Lay lemon slices on top of fish and cook until fish is done (about 45 minutes), shaking pan slightly a few times and basting occasionally. If fish sticks to pan, it can easily be lifted out with 2 pancake turners, using one at each end of the fish. Place on platter, pour sauce over, and serve. Serves 6-8.

Baked Fish Slices

4-6 slices cod, halibut, or sole
⅓-½ cup mayonnaise
⅓   cup cracker meal
      salt, pepper to taste

Season fish slices with salt and pepper. Spread mayonnaise on both sides of slices and dip into cracker meal. Bake in 400 degree oven on cookie sheet for 20-30 minutes, or until fish is tender. Cooking time will depend upon the thickness of the slices.

Steamed Clams

3   dozen clams, well-cleaned
4   tablespoons butter
2   cloves garlic, chopped fine
2   tablespoons parsley
½   cup water
      dash or two of pepper

Melt butter in pot; add garlic, parsley and pepper and stir until well-blended. Add water and clams and cover pot. Let steam over low heat, shaking pot occasionally, until shells open, about 15-20 minutes. Serve clams in their shells in soup plates and pour broth over them, or broth can be served separately in a cup. Serves 4.

Baked Clams

1 lb. clams, chopped
1 big onion, chopped fine
4 tablespoons parsley, chopped fine
2 tablespoons olive oil
2 tablespoons butter
2 slices bacon, fried crisp and chopped
5-6 slices bread, soaked in milk and squeezed dry
1 8 oz. can tomato sauce
½ cup buttered soda cracker crumbs
½ cup grated Parmesan cheese
   salt, pepper to taste

Brown onion and parsley in oil and butter. Add clams, bacon, and bread. Salt and pepper to taste, then add tomato sauce. Bake in ramekins or clam shells, topping each with a sprinkling of cracker crumbs. Bake ½ hour at 350 degrees. Sprinkle with grated cheese before serving. Serves 6-8.

Rice and Clams

2 tablespoons oil
6-8 tablespoons butter
1 onion, chopped
4 cloves garlic, pressed
2 tablespoons chopped parsley
1 sprig thyme, chopped, or
   ¼ teaspoon dry thyme
¼ cup dry Italian mushrooms, cut into pieces
1 8 oz. can tomato sauce
⅔ cup August Sebastiani Chablis or Country French Colombard
4 cups water
2 cups uncooked rice
3 dozen clams (in shells)
   salt, pepper to taste
   grated Parmesan cheese

Sauté onion in oil and butter over low heat. Sprinkle generously with salt and pepper and stir frequently. Add garlic, parsley, thyme, and stir. Add tomato sauce, wine, and water. Cover and simmer for 20 minutes. Add rice and mix together well. Add more water if necessary and a dash of salt. Stir frequently to prevent rice from sticking and cook uncovered until rice is almost cooked, about 20 minutes. Salt to taste at this point. Add clams and stir. Cover again and let steam on slow fire until clams have opened. Stir occasionally and serve with grated cheese. Serves 6.

Be sure to wash clams well to remove all sand. When serving, place soup bowls on dinner table for empty clam shells and have plenty of napkins on hand as fingers are a must for eating clams.

Filets Florentine

2 lbs. spinach or 2 packages
    frozen chopped spinach
4 tablespoons butter
½ cup water
½ cup Sebastiani Chardonnay
3 peppercorns
1 small onion stuck with 1 clove
1 sprig parsley
4 fish filets
2 tablespoons flour
½ cup heavy cream
    few grains nutmeg
    few drops lemon juice
    grated Parmesan cheese
    salt, pepper to taste

Cook spinach, drain well, and chop very fine. Season to taste with 2 tablespoons butter, salt, and pepper. Arrange on a well-buttered oval baking dish and keep warm. Combine water with wine, pepper corns, onion, parsley, and more salt and pepper to taste. Bring to a boil and let cook 5 minutes. Add fish and simmer until fish is cooked through, about 5 minutes longer. Remove fish to a hot plate; let liquid simmer 2-3 minutes longer and strain. Melt 2 tablespoons butter in a separate saucepan and blend well with flour. Stirring constantly, gradually add strained broth from the fish. Continue stirring until thick. Add cream, nutmeg, and lemon juice. Place cooked fish filets on bed of spinach, cover with wine sauce, and sprinkle liberally with cheese. Place dish in 450 degree oven for 5 minutes until cheese is delicately browned. Serves 4.

Stuffed Filets of Sole

½ teaspoon minced onion
1 teaspoon celery, minced
1 tablespoon butter or oil
½ cup bread crumbs
1 egg
1 small can shrimp, chopped
8 medium filets of sole
½ cup milk
1 can cream of mushroom soup
½ lb. or 1 small can crab meat
    salt, and white pepper to taste
    paprika

Sauté onion and celery lightly in butter or oil. Add bread crumbs, salt, and other seasoning if desired. Cool; add egg and shrimp. Place 1 tablespoon of this mixture on each filet and roll. Fasten with toothpick and place fish in baking dish. Mix milk with soup and half the crab. Pour over filets and top with remaining crab. Sprinkle with paprika. Bake in 325 degree oven for 30 minutes. Serves 8.

Fried Oysters

2 dozen medium oysters
2 eggs
½ package cracker crumbs
4 tablespoons olive oil
2 tablespoons butter
   salt, pepper, garlic salt to taste
   lemon wedges

Wash oysters well, rinse, and dry thoroughly. Beat eggs, then dip in oysters. Roll in cracker crumbs and fry in oil and butter. Season to taste. Serve with lemon wedges. Serves 4-6.

Creamed Tuna

2 tablespoons butter
2 tablespoons flour
1 cup hot milk
⅛ teaspoon pepper
¼ teaspoon salt
1 teaspoon Worcestershire sauce
1 can pimiento, diced
1 can sliced mushrooms with liquid
   (optional)
¼ cup Sebastiani "Eye of the Swan"
   Pinot Noir Blanc or August
   Sebastiani Country Chardonnay
1 13 oz. can tuna

Melt butter in top of double boiler. Add flour and mix well. Then add milk, pepper, and salt and stir until thick. Add Worcestershire, pimiento, mushrooms, and wine. Stir, then add tuna, broken into pieces. Continue to cook, stirring occasionally, until heated thoroughly. Serves 4-6.

Suggestions

1. In meat dishes that call for wine, always heat wine first before adding. If cold wine is used, it tends to make the meat tough.

2. When oil is called for in a recipe, a good grade of olive oil should be used.

3. It's better not to buy ready-ground hamburger. There is a high percentage of fat and gristle in this meat which is rapidly cooked away and leaves very little actual meat. Buy ground round or chuck if you can.

4. Always trim off excess fat from meats.

5. Fresh herbs have more flavor than dry herbs and should be used at all times if available. This is especially true when cooking meats and you will find your meats have a much better flavor cooked with fresh herbs. Perhaps you could grow your own herbs in a window box or garden.

6. If you do buy prepared herbs, be sure to choose chopped herbs and not the powdered type.

Boiled Italian Sausage and Potatoes

4   Italian sausages
2   medium potatoes, cut in half
    olive oil
    vinegar
    salt, pepper to taste

Prick skins of sausages with a fork in several places. Place sausage along with potatoes in skillet and cover with boiling water. Cook until potatoes are tender, about 20-30 minutes. Drain well and cut sausage into 1½ inch pieces. Cut potatoes into smaller pieces and marinate with oil and vinegar, adding salt and pepper to taste. Serve hot.

Boiled Beef

1   2-2½ lb. boneless rump roast or
    chuck roast, trimmed of fat
2   onions
2   carrots
2   stalks celery
4-5 sprigs parsley
1   tablespoon salt
3-4 peppercorns
2   cloves garlic

Place meat in a soup pot and add enough cold water to cover completely. Add salt, bring to a boil over high heat, skimming surface when foam rises. Reduce heat and partially cover. Cook for 1 hour. Add vegetables and cook 1 hour longer or until meat is tender. Remove meat to carving board and cut into slices. Arrange on platter and surround with carrots and onions. Strain broth and serve as soup with a fine pasta in it. Serves 6.

Joe's Special

1   small onion, chopped
2   tablespoons oil
1   tablespoon butter
1   lb. ground beef
    salt, pepper, garlic salt to taste
1   clove garlic, pressed
¼   cup August Sebastiani Chablis or
    Country White Zinfandel
1   package frozen spinach, chopped
3   tablespoons grated Parmesan cheese
1   4 oz. can sliced mushrooms,
    drained (optional)
2   eggs

Sauté onion slightly with oil and butter; add ground beef. Sprinkle salt, pepper, and garlic salt over meat while browning, then add garlic and sauté lightly. Add wine. Add spinach, stirring frequently until thawed out and cooked. Blend cheese in well, then add mushrooms. Mix in eggs a few minutes before serving. Serves 4-5 with very generous helpings.

If available, a link of Italian sausage adds zest to this dish. Simply break it up into very small pieces and add it to the beef prior to browning. A Sebastiani dry Red wine is a must with this dish.

Easy Chuck Roast

4   tablespoons oil
2   tablespoons butter
1   chuck roast
     salt, pepper, and garlic powder
     to taste
1   can mushroom soup, undiluted
1   can onion soup, undiluted
1   cup Sebastiani Zinfandel or
     Pinot Noir

Melt oil and butter in Dutch oven on top of stove. Brown roast well on both sides, seasoning well with salt, pepper, and garlic powder. Mix together soups and wine, add to roast and cover. Bake at 350 degrees for 2½ hours. Turn at least 2 or 3 times while baking.

Brains and Eggs

2   sets calf brains
4   or 5 eggs
     salt, pepper to taste

Remove membranes from outsides of brains and wash thoroughly. Put brains in boiling water for 15 minutes. Remove and cut into 1 inch chunks. Mix brains with eggs that have been seasoned with salt and pepper. Fry as you would scrambled eggs. Serves 4.

Calf Brains

2   sets calf brains
1   egg
½   cup cracker meal
     salt, pepper to taste
     lemon wedges

Remove membrane from outsides of brains and wash thoroughly. Drain or pat dry with a paper towel. Beat egg with a fork and roll brains in egg and then in the cracker meal that has been mixed with salt and pepper. In a well-greased pan, bake at 350 degrees, turning when brown, and cook for a total of 25 minutes. Serve with lemon wedges. Serves 4.

Corned Beef

1	package corned beef
1½	cups August Sebastiani Burgundy or Country Zinfandel
2	bay leaves
3-4	peppercorns
1	clove garlic
1	small onion

In a deep saucepan, place the corned beef and add wine. Add enough water to cover. Add bay leaves, peppercorns, garlic, and onion and simmer according to directions given on the package of corned beef.

Corned Beef and Cabbage

1	package corned beef
2	bay leaves
3-4	peppercorns
1	clove garlic
3	onions
2-3	peeled potatoes, cut in half
3	carrots (optional)
1	head cabbage, cut into wedges

In a deep saucepan, place the corned beef and add enough water to cover. Add bay leaves, peppercorns, and garlic and simmer according to directions given on the package of corned beef. Add onions, potatoes, and carrots half an hour before cooking time is completed and add cabbage for the last 15 minutes of cooking. Serve the beef surrounded by the vegetables and use mustard as a condiment.

Sebastiani Burgundy serves as a fine accompaniment to this dish.

Champagne Ham

1	7-8 lb. canned ham
3	cups champagne
	Karo syrup

Marinate ham in champagne for 8 hours, turning frequently. Bake in a 300 degree oven for 1 hour, basting often with champagne. After 1 hour, score top of ham and brush well with syrup. Bake ham for 30 minutes longer; slice as thinly as possible and serve.

Flaming Ham

1	6-7 lb. ham
1⅓	cup brown sugar
2	tablespoons flour
½	teaspoon ground cloves
2	tablespoons water
2	tablespoons orange extract
½	cup warm brandy

Bake ham, following directions on can. Mix 1 cup sugar, flour, and cloves moistened with water. Use this as a glaze during the last 30 minutes of baking. When ham is done, transfer to a platter and pat on remaining brown sugar, mixed with orange extract. Carry ham to table and ignite. Then spoon over warm brandy to extend the flaming time. Serves 10-12.

Ham Loaf

1	lb. uncooked ham, ground
½	lb. lean ground pork
1	egg, slightly beaten
½	cup milk
½	cup cracker or bread crumbs
½	teaspoon paprika
½	teaspoon salt
½	onion, grated
½	cup tomato soup

Combine ham and pork. Mix egg, milk, crumbs, and remaining ingredients together. Add to meat and blend well. Bake in 350 degree oven 45-50 minutes. Top with sauce before serving. Serves 6.

Sauce:

1	tablespoon butter
1	tablespoon flour
¼	cup sugar
1	teaspoon dry mustard
¼	cup vinegar
1½	cups tomato juice
1	egg, slightly beaten

Melt butter; add flour and stir well. Add remaining ingredients, the egg last, and cook until thick.

Glazed Ham

1	3-4 lb. canned ham
1½	cups August Sebastiani Country Chenin Blanc or Country Chardonnay
½	cup brown sugar

Place ham in shallow baking pan; pour over 1 cup wine and bake 1 hour at 325 degrees. Combine brown sugar with remaining wine. Cook, stirring constantly, until thick. Baste ham occasionally with this mixture during an additional half hour of cooking. You may need to add a little water while baking if the pan gets dry. Serves 6-8.

Kidneys

6   lamb or 4 veal kidneys
     salted water
2   tablespoons vinegar
2   tablespoons olive oil
½   onion, chopped
1   clove garlic, chopped
½   teaspoon parsley
¼   cup August Sebastiani Chablis
     or Country Chardonnay
     salt, pepper to taste

Plunge kidneys in boiling water. Remove skins and soak in cold salted water to which vinegar has been added for 30 minutes. Slice kidneys thin, removing tubes and tissues and season with salt and pepper. Heat oil in a frying pan and add onion, garlic, and parsley, sautéing lightly for 2 minutes. Then add kidneys and fry over high heat for a few minutes. Do not overcook as it makes kidneys tough. Add hot wine, stir once, and serve immediately. Serves 4-6.

Roast Lamb Shanks

2   lamb shanks
     salt, pepper, garlic salt to taste
2   bell peppers
2   white onions
1   medium size potato, cut into
     quarters
½   teaspoon thyme
½   cup Sebastiani Chardonnay
     or August Sebastiani Country
     Fumé Blanc

Season · shanks generously with salt, pepper, and garlic salt. Halve bell peppers and onions and place in a greased roasting pan along with the shanks and potato pieces. Season to taste. Bake at 350 degrees for 1½ hours. Add wine when meat has browned and is nearly done. If meat becomes cooked before potato pieces, remove meat from pan and wrap in foil to keep warm. Add meat to rest of mixture before serving. Serves 2.

Roast Leg of Lamb

1   leg of lamb
1   lemon
2   cloves garlic, pressed
¼   cup olive oil
½   cup August Sebastiani Country
     Chardonnay or Country
     White Zinfandel
3-4   potatoes, quartered
4   green peppers, left whole or
     cut in half
6   small onions
6   carrots, cut in half (optional)
     salt, pepper to taste

Cut lemon in half and rub the lamb with the juice. Salt and pepper generously and spread garlic on all sides. Put lamb into large shallow roasting pan with oil and wine. Bake at 325 degrees, basting occasionally. After 1 hour, add potatoes, peppers, onions, and carrots that have been seasoned with additional salt and pepper. Add more oil if necessary to prevent drying. Turn vegetables gently while cooking; if potatoes cook before other vegetables, remove and keep hot. Total cooking time about 2½ hours.

Meat Loaf

1	lb. ground beef
½	cup oatmeal (quick type)
1	small onion, chopped fine
1	clove garlic, pressed
4	tablespoons grated Parmesan cheese
2	teaspoons chopped parsley
1	8 oz. can tomato sauce
3	tablespoons August Sebastiani Country Cabernet Sauvignon or Country Pinot Noir
1	teaspoon salt
½	teaspoon pepper
½	teaspoon garlic salt
1	egg, beaten

Combine all ingredients, using only three-fourths of the tomato sauce. Shape into a greased loaf pan and pour remaining tomato sauce over loaf. Bake for 1 hour at 350 degrees.

Instead of the chopped onion, half package of Lipton Onion Soup mix can be used. If you use the soup mix, reduce the amount of salt to half teaspoon.

Pork Loin Roast

1	pork loin roast
	salt
	pepper
2	cloves garlic, pressed
1	cup Sebastiani "Eye of the Swan" Pinot Noir Blanc or Chardonnay
½	cup water

Season roast with salt and pepper and rub with garlic. Place in roasting pan with wine and water. Bake at 325 degrees for 2-2½ hours, basting and turning occasionally. When roast is cooked, there should be enough liquid to add to the meat when it is served. If, while roasting, it looks as though there isn't enough liquid, add more wine.

Baked Spareribs

1	side spareribs, about 2 lbs.
	salt
	pepper
	garlic salt
	soy sauce
	paprika

Cut spareribs into small pieces and sprinkle on both sides with remaining ingredients. Place on broiler pan and bake at 350 degrees for 1 hour. Turn at least one time while baking.

Osso Buco

6 veal marrowbones with their meat, cut into pieces 3 inches long
4 tablespoons butter
4 tablespoons oil
1 small grated carrot
⅓ cup chopped celery
1 medium onion, chopped
1 clove garlic, chopped
  pinch of rosemary
  pinch of sage
4 tablespoons tomato sauce
1 cup August Sebastiani Chablis or Country Chardonnay
½ cup water
  salt, pepper to taste

Brown veal in butter and oil, seasoning with salt and pepper. Brown on all sides, then turn pieces upright to hold in marrow. Add carrot, celery, onion, garlic, rosemary, and sage. Cover pot and simmer 10 minutes. Blend tomato sauce with wine and stir into veal. Add water and simmer over low heat, adding small amounts of water if necessary to prevent drying. Simmer until meat is tender, about 2 hours. Serve over boiled rice if desired.

I suggest Sebastiani Barbera with this dish

Veal Scallopine

1½ lbs. veal scallops, cut ⅜ inch thick and pounded until ¼ inch thick
¼ teaspoon sage or 2 leaves fresh sage
  salt, pepper to taste
  flour
2 tablespoons butter
4 tablespoons olive oil
¾ cup Sebastiani Chardonnay or August Sebastiani Country Fumé Blanc
1 small can button mushrooms, liquid included (if you like mushrooms, use a larger can)
  juice of 1 lemon
4 tablespoons chopped parsley

Season veal with sage, salt, and pepper. Dip in flour and shake off excess. In a heavy skillet, melt butter with oil. Add veal, 4-5 scallops at a time, and sauté them about 2 minutes on each side until they are golden brown. Transfer scallops to a plate. Pour off almost all fat from the skillet, leaving only a thin film on the bottom. Add wine, mushrooms, lemon juice, and parsley, and boil briskly 1-2 minutes, stirring constantly. Scrape any browned bits clinging to the skillet. Return veal to skillet. Cover and simmer 10-15 minutes until veal is tender when pierced with the tip of a sharp knife. Serves 4.

Saltimbocca

8   thin veal cutlets
     salt, pepper, powdered sage
     to taste
4   thin slices proscuitto (Italian ham)
4   thin slices Fontina cheese
4   tablespoons oil
6   tablespoons butter
8   fresh mushrooms, sliced or 1
     8 oz. can mushrooms with liquid
4   teaspoons parsley, chopped fine
1   clove garlic, pressed
1½   cups August Sebastiani Country
     Chardonnay or Country Chenin
     Blanc

Season each cutlet with salt, pepper, and sage. On top of four cutlets, layer ham and cheese and top with remaining cutlets. The veal should cover the ham and cheese completely. Press edges of the veal together and seal by pounding with the flat of a cleaver. Secure with wooden picks. Brown both sides well in heated oil and 2 tablespoons butter, seasoning as you wish. Remove and place into a shallow heated roasting pan. In a separate pan, sauté mushrooms, parsley, and garlic in butter. Add wine to the pan in which the veal was browned and simmer a few minutes. Add mushrooms and parsley and pour over meat. Add 4 tablespoons butter and cook until tender. Serves 4.

Another method is to roll the veal slices after placing seasonings and ham on them (eliminating the cheese) with the veal on the outside, and fasten the rolls with toothpicks. Sauté the rolls in butter and olive oil until they are thoroughly brown. Add white wine to the pan and simmer until veal is tender. Remove the toothpicks and serve the rolls on a heated platter with the sauce poured over them.

Short Ribs of Beef

4	short ribs
4	tablespoons oil
2	tablespoons butter
	salt, pepper, garlic salt to taste
1	onion, chopped
1	18 oz. can solid pack tomatoes with liquid
½	cup August Sebastiani Country Cabernet Sauvignon or Country Pinot Noir
	teaspoon paprika

In a deep casserole, add oil, butter and short ribs that have been well-seasoned with salt, pepper, and garlic salt. Turn ribs so that they brown well on all sides. Add onion and stir until slightly brown. Then add tomatoes, wine, and paprika. Cover and place in 325 degree oven. Cook 2-3 hours until short ribs are tender when tested with a fork. Turn 2-3 times while baking. If short ribs seem dry, add a little water during cooking.

Baked Chuck Roast

1	chuck roast, 2-3 lbs.
1	clove garlic, pressed
	salt, pepper to taste
1	package Lipton Onion Soup mix
2	potatoes
2-3	carrots
¼	cup Sebastiani Cabernet Sauvignon or August Sebastiani Country Pinot Noir

Line sides and bottom of a shallow roasting pan with heavy aluminum foil. Rub roast with garlic and season with salt and pepper. Place meat on foil and spread soup mix over same. Peel and cut potatoes and carrots into good-sized chunks and place around roast. Salt and pepper vegetables. Take ends of foil and bring up over meat and vegetables. Pour wine over roast, then fold foil to keep it closed. Bake for 2-2½ hours at 350 degrees. Serves 6.

This is a meal in itself—all that is needed to accompany this dish is a green salad. I have served this to guests, including the chef of one of Sonoma County's leading restaurants, adding sliced cooked mushrooms on top...no one believed it was a chuck roast!

Sima (Stuffed Breast of Veal)

1	breast or shoulder of veal with a pocket cut in
1	onion, chopped
4	tablespoons oil
2	tablespoons butter
2	cloves garlic, pressed
2	packages frozen chopped spinach or 2 bunches fresh spinach—well-cooked, drained, and chopped fine
½	cup chopped parsley
5	eggs
2	cups bread crumbs
¾	cup grated Parmesan cheese
	dash of basil
	salt, pepper to taste
1	teaspoon rosemary
1	cup Sebastiani "Eye of the Swan" Pinot Noir Blanc or August Sebastiani Country Chardonnay
⅓	cup butter

Sauté onion in oil and butter, adding 1 clove garlic last. Add spinach, parsley, eggs, bread crumbs, cheese, and seasonings, mixing well with a fork. Stuff into pocket in veal and sew with a coarse needle and thread, closing completely. Place in roasting pan and rub with 1 clove garlic. Sprinkle with rosemary and baste with wine and butter. Roast uncovered at 350 degrees until brown, about 1 hour, basting occasionally. Serves 6-8.

Stuffed Flank Steak

1	flank steak, pounded so that it is thin enough to roll
1½	cups sliced fresh mushrooms or canned mushrooms
4	tablespoons butter
	salt, pepper, garlic powder to taste
1½	cups August Sebastiani Chablis or Country Chardonnay
	flour
4	tablespoons oil
½	cup water
	bread stuffing (see recipe under miscellaneous. Add 4 tablespoons pork sausage meat and 1 egg)

Sauté mushrooms in 2 tablespoons butter with salt, pepper, and garlic powder to taste. Add ½ cup wine and simmer about 20 minutes. Season meat on all sides with salt, pepper, and garlic powder, then spread with stuffing. Roll lengthwise and tie securely with string about 2 inches apart. Dust roll generously with flour and brown well in oil and remaining butter. Add water and remaining wine, cover and simmer, turning occasionally, for about 1 hour or until tender when tested with a fork. Remove roll from pan and cool slightly so that when you slice it about 1 inch thick, the roll will stay together. Serve with a little gravy and sliced mushrooms.

Swiss Steak

2 lbs. round steak
   flour
2 tablespoons oil
2 tablespoons butter
3 stalks celery, chopped
2 cloves garlic, pressed
1 small green pepper, cut in pieces
1 medium onion, chopped
1 teaspoon oregano
2 tablespoons chopped parsley
1 small can tomato sauce
1 cup August Sebastiani Country
   Cabernet Sauvignon or
   Country Pinot Noir
   salt, pepper to taste
1 can ripe olives

Cut steak as desired, then pound with flour that has been seasoned with salt and pepper. Brown in a Dutch oven, seasoning to taste. Remove meat and add celery, garlic, green pepper, onion, oregano, and parsley. Sauté lightly, then return meat and add tomato sauce. Cover with wine. Simmer 1½ hours over low heat until meat is tender, then add olives and cook about 10 minutes longer. Serve over cooked rice. Serves 4-6.

Tongue

1 beef tongue
2 bay leaves
1 onion
4 cloves
1 red chili pepper
1 tablespoon salt
6 peppercorns
   oil, vinegar, salt, pepper, chopped
   parsley, and garlic to taste

Wash tongue thoroughly and put in a large pot. Add bay leaves, onion, cloves, peppercorns and salt. Add enough cold water just to cover meat and bring liquid to a slow boil, skimming frequently. Simmer covered over low heat for 3 hours until tongue is tender. Let tongue cool in water. Drain, peel off skin, and trim gristle and root away. Slice thin and serve cold with oil, vinegar, salt, pepper, chopped parsley and garlic to taste.

Tongue and Spanish Sauce

1 beef tongue, cooked as in
   recipe given above.
4 tablespoons oil
2 tablespoons butter
1 small dried onion, chopped
1 clove garlic, chopped
3 stalks celery, chopped
1 green pepper, chopped
1 small red chili pepper,
   chopped (optional)
1 16 oz. can tomatoes, chopped
½ cup August Sebastiani Chablis
   or Country Chardonnay
   salt, pepper to taste

In deep pan, heat oil and butter. Add onions and brown, sprinkling with salt and pepper. Add garlic, peppers, celery, tomatoes, and wine. More salt and pepper may be added to suit your taste. Simmer 45 minutes to 1 hour. Then add sliced tongue and heat thoroughly.

This can be made up a day ahead as it is much better when re-heated.

Tripe

1½-2 lbs. tripe
4 tablespoons oil
2 tablespoons butter
1 onion, chopped
1 clove garlic, chopped
2 teaspoons chopped parsley
¼ cup dried Italian mushrooms
   (optional)
1 8 oz. can tomato sauce
   dash of cayenne pepper
1 cup August Sebastiani Chablis
   or Country Chardonnay
1 medium potato, cut into ½ inch cubes
   salt, pepper to taste
   grated Parmesan cheese

Cut tripe into strips 3 inches long and ½ inch wide. In a saucepan, heat oil and butter and sauté onion, taking care not to let it brown. Add salt and pepper to taste. Add garlic, parsley, mushrooms, and tomato sauce. Put tripe into saucepan and add wine. Add enough water to cover tripe completely. Stir all ingredients and cover after adding dash of cayenne pepper. Simmer for 1½ hours; then add potato and continue cooking until potato and tripe are tender. Sprinkle with cheese when serving. Serves 6-8.

Sebastiani Burgundy goes especially well with this dish.

Breaded Veal Cutlets

6 veal steaks or chops
2 eggs, beaten with a fork
   cracker crumbs mixed with 3
   tablespoons grated Parmesan
   cheese
   salt, pepper, garlic salt to taste
4 tablespoons olive oil
2 tablespoons butter
   lemon wedges

Season steaks or chops generously with salt, pepper, and garlic salt. Dip into eggs, then dip into seasoned cracker crumbs. Place in shallow baking dish along with oil and butter. Brown at 350 degrees until tender, turning once so that both sides are browned. Takes about 15-20 minutes on each side. Serve with lemon wedges.

Veal Sautéed with Olives

1½ lbs. veal, cut like stew meat
4 tablespoons olive oil
2 tablespoons butter
   salt, pepper, galic salt to taste
1 clove garlic, pressed
2 teaspoons chopped parsley
¼ teaspoon sage
¾ cup Sebastiani Sauvignon Blanc
   or August Sebastiani Country
   Chardonnay
½ cup hard green olives

Brown veal in oil and butter, adding salt, pepper, and garlic salt to all sides. Turn frequently with spatula until brown. Add garlic, parsley, sage, and heated wine. Add olives and cover. Simmer for 20 minutes or until veal is tender. You may add more wine if you wish the veal to be more moist.

Cappretto (kid goat) is good cooked this way, too. Sometimes I use the dark dry olives in place of the green.

Veal Parmigiano

4-6 veal steaks, round
2   eggs, beaten
⅔   cup cracker meal
4   tablespoons oil
2   tablespoons butter
4   tablespoons grated Parmesan
     cheese
     spaghetti sauce (see recipe in
     this book)
4   tablespoons August Sebastiani Chablis
     or Country Chardonnay
4-6 slices Monterey cheese
     salt, pepper to taste

Dip veal steaks into eggs, adding salt and pepper. After this, dip into cracker meal on both sides. Brown veal on both sides in oil and butter, adding salt and pepper to both sides. Place in shallow baking pan, sprinkle with Parmesan, and cover with sauce. Bake at 325 degrees for 30 minutes or until veal is tender. Just before serving, add a slice of Monterey cheese over each steak. More sauce may be added if desired. Serves 4-6.

Veal Paprika in Noodle Ring

4   lbs. veal shoulder, cut into 1½ inch
      cubes
¼   cup butter
¼   cup oil
2   teaspoons salt
1   tablespoon sugar
4   teaspoons curry powder
1¼   teaspoons pepper
¼   teaspoon paprika
1   10½ oz. can condensed beef
      broth, undiluted
2½   cups sour cream
⅔   cup flour
⅔   cup cold water
1   cup snipped parsley
1   8 oz. package broad noodles
¼   cup toasted slivered almonds
1½   teaspoons poppy seed

About 2 hours before dinner, brown ⅓ of the veal cubes in hot butter and oil. Remove to plate and repeat twice more. Combine in dutch oven and sprinkle with salt, sugar, curry, pepper, and paprika. Add broth, sour cream, and stir in flour that has previously been blended smooth with water; add parsley. Simmer with cover on for 1 hour, stirring occasionally until veal is tender. Cook noodles as directed on package and let drain well. About 30 minutes before dinner, heat oven to 350 degrees. Arrange cooked noodles in ring around edge of a shallow baking dish. Spoon veal mixture into center and top with almonds and poppy seeds. Cover with foil and bake 15 minutes. Serves 8.

Poultry

Chicken Almond

4 lbs. chicken breasts or
   2 broilers, cut up
   flour seasoned with salt and pepper
4 tablespoons oil
2 tablespoons butter
2 onions, chopped
2 green peppers, chopped
1 clove garlic, chopped
3½ teaspoons curry powder
½ teaspoon white pepper
½ teaspoon thyme
1 28 oz. can solid pack tomatoes, mashed
1 tablespoon chopped parsley
¼ cup toasted almonds
¾ cup August Sebastiani Chablis
   or Country French Colombard
6 cups cooked rice

Roll chicken in seasoned flour and brown in oil and butter. Remove chicken pieces. Add onions, peppers, and garlic, stirring well and adding salt and pepper to taste. Then add tomatoes and parsley and heat thoroughly. Place in a greased casserole dish and add almonds and wine, mixing well. Cover and bake at 350 degrees for 45 minutes. Serve over rice. Serves 8.

Chicken Cacciatore a la Lombarda

1 chicken, cut into pieces
2 tablespoons flour
4 tablespoons olive oil
2 tablespoons butter
   salt, pepper to taste
½ onion, chopped
1 stalk celery, chopped
1 clove garlic, pressed
1 tablespoon chopped parsley
1 small can sliced button mushrooms
1½ cups August Sebastiani Chablis
   or Country Chardonnay
½ teaspoon thyme
½ teaspoon rosemary

Dust chicken lightly with flour. Brown well in oil and butter, sprinkling all sides with salt and pepper while cooking. Add chopped onion and celery: salt and pepper to taste. Stir frequently with pancake turner until celery and onion are limp. Then add garlic and parsley, stirring constantly. Add mushrooms, wine, thyme, and rosemary. Cover and simmer for about 45 minutes. If there seems to be too much liquid, cook without cover for the last 10-15 minutes. Serves 4-6.

Pheasant can also be prepared according to this recipe. Cooking time will depend upon the size and age of the pheasant; it may take anywhere from 1-2 hours. This cacciatore dish goes well with polenta (see recipe in the Miscellaneous section of this book). Serve over polenta and top all with grated Parmesan cheese.

Chicken Bordeaux

1   fryer, cut up
2   tablespoons butter
2   tablespoons olive oil
    salt, pepper to taste
1   tablespoon chopped parsley
2   cloves garlic, pressed
1   tablespoon minced onion
1   cup August Sebastiani Country
    Chardonnay or Country Fumé Blanc
1   package frozen artichoke hearts
1   6 oz. can whole mushrooms with
    liquid

Heat together butter and oil and cook chicken pieces until golden brown, seasoning well with salt and pepper. Sprinkle with parsley, then cover and cook slowly 8-9 minutes. Remove chicken pieces and keep warm. Add garlic, onion, wine, artichokes, and mushrooms to the juices in the pan. Bring to a boil and cook 1 minute longer. Return chicken to pan, reheat, and serve immediately. Serves 4-6.

Chicken in Sherry Sauce

6   chicken breasts
    salt, pepper to taste
½   cup Dry Sherry or Cream Sherry
1   can cream of mushroom soup
½   pt. sour cream

Sprinkle chicken with salt and pepper and lay in baking pan. Mix well wine, soup, and sour cream and pour over chicken. Bake for 1 hour and 10 minutes in 350 degree oven. Serves 6.
Note: If you don't have any Sherry, Sebastiani Vineyards Chenin Blanc or August Sebastiani Country Chenin Blanc can be used.

Chicken with Wine and Mushrooms

1   fryer, cut up
    salt, pepper, garlic salt, paprika
    to taste
4   tablespoons butter
6   tablespoons olive oil
1   can sliced, button mushrooms,
    with liquid
¾   cup Sebastiani Chardonnay or
    Sauvignon Blanc
1 or 2 clove garlic, chopped (optional)
2 or 3 sprigs rosemary (optional)

Season chicken pieces generously with salt, pepper, garlic salt, and paprika. Melt butter and oil in shallow roasting pan and place chicken pieces in pan. Place pan in 350 degree oven and turn pieces as they brown. Heat mushrooms with liquid in wine. After 30 minutes, add to chicken. If desired, garlic and rosemary may be added, but remove before serving. Continue cooking until tender, about 15-20 minutes. Serves 4-6.

Chilied Chicken

4   large chicken breasts, boned
      and cut up
1   package tortillas
⅔   cup milk
1   can diced Oretega chilies
1   small onion, chopped
1   can cream of chicken soup
1   can cream of mushroom soup
1   can chopped olives
¾   lb. Tillamook cheese

Soak tortillas in milk. Make sauce by mixing chilies, onion, soups, olives, and cheese. Add chicken pieces. Drain tortillas. Layer tortillas and chicken mixture in a greased casserole dish. If desired, the milk from the tortillas may be mixed with the chili sauce. Bake at 350 degrees for 30 minutes. Serves 4.

Nona's Chicken

2   chickens, cut into large pieces
      flour
      salt
      pepper
      garlic salt
2   tablespoons olive oil
6   tablespoons butter
½   cup chopped parsley
1   can sliced mushrooms, drained
      (optional)
⅛   teaspoon red chili peppers,
      minced
      rosemary
      thyme
1   cup August Sebastiani Chablis
      or Country Chardonnay

Season chicken with salt, pepper, and garlic salt. Dust lightly with flour, then place pieces in shallow baking pan or on cookie sheet, sprinkling over oil and melted butter. Brown chicken under broiler, turning all sides to brown. After browning, layer pieces in a deep, greased casserole, sprinkling each layer with parsley, mushrooms, chili peppers, rosemary, thyme, and salt and pepper to taste. Pour over remaining pan juices and wine. Cover and bake at 325 degrees for 1-1½ hours until chicken is tender. Serves 10-12.

Sebastiani Country Chardonnay (chilled) goes especially well with this chicken dish.

Chicken Giblet Sauté

1½   lbs. chicken giblets
1   tablespoon flour
½   teaspoon salt
      pepper to taste
1   tablespoon butter
2   tablespoons olive oil
1   clove garlic, pressed
1   cup August Sebastiani Chablis
      or Country Fumé Blanc
½   cup water
1   small can mushrooms (optional)
      grated Parmesan cheese (optional)

Roll giblets in flour that has been seasoned with salt and pepper. Melt butter with oil in a saucepan and add giblets, stirring well. Sauté giblets until brown, then add water, wine and mushrooms. Cover and stir occasionally until tender, about 25-30 minutes. More salt and wine may be added if needed. Sprinkle with cheese before serving over boiled rice or noodles. Serves 4.

Roast Chicken

1   chicken, any size (roaster)
      salt, pepper, garlic salt to taste
1   sprig thyme
1   sprig rosemary
1   clove garlic, mashed
½   dry onion, cut into 4 pieces
1-1½ cups Sebastiani Chardonnay

Sprinkle chicken generously with salt, pepper, and garlic salt. Be sure to cover all sides and in the cavity. Place thyme, rosemary, garlic, and onion inside chicken. Place in shallow roasting pan with a little oil and butter. Cook at 350 degrees and baste occasionally until slightly brown, about 30 minutes. Then add wine that has been heated, not boiled, and baste occasionally until done. A 4 lb. chicken will take about 1 hour and 15 minutes.

Turkey and Turkey Dressing

1   roasting turkey
      dry bread cubes from 1 loaf of
      sour French bread
½   cup chopped parsley
½   cup grated Parmesan cheese
1 or 2 teaspoons poultry seasoning
2   teaspoons salt
1   teaspoon pepper
1   teaspoon garlic salt
½   cup butter
2   onions, chopped
½   bunch celery, chopped
2   cloves garlic, chopped
1-2 cups broth

Broth:
      turkey neck
      turkey giblets
      salted water
¼   onion
1   stalk celery
1   clove garlic
1½   cups Sebastiani Chenin Blanc
      or Chardonnay
1½   cups melted butter

In a large bowl, combine bread cubes, parsley, cheese, and seasonings. In melted butter, sauté onion, and celery, sprinkling with salt, pepper, and garlic salt to taste. Add garlic and sauté lightly. Prepare broth by boiling neck and giblets in salted water with onion, celery, and garlic. Let cool. Add cooled broth to onion-celery mixture, then mix well into bread cube mixture.

Rub turkey with olive oil and season generouly with salt, pepper, and garlic salt. Stuff with dressing. When turkey is ready for baking, place in a shallow oiled roasting pan and baste occasionally while cooking with wine and butter. Cook at 325 degrees. Turkey is cooked when leg joints move freely. Remove from oven and let sit at least 1 hour before carving. Cover with foil to keep warm. This procedure makes it much easier to carve the turkey and keeps the meat moist.

When I start to roast a turkey, I like to cover it with a large, heavy paper shopping bag. Simply cut out one side of the bag and place over turkey. This produces a very golden finish on the bird.

Game

Cornish Game Hen in Casserole

6   game hens, split
¼   cup flour
4   tablespoons butter
4   tablespoons olive oil
1   cup chicken broth
1   can cream of chicken soup
½   cup Sebastiani Johannisberg Riesling or August Sebastiani Country Chenin Blanc
1   cup sour cream
    pepper to taste

Dust game hens with flour and sauté in butter and oil for 10 minutes or until brown. Remove from skillet and arrange in casserole dish. Add chicken broth to butter and oil in skillet, stir well, and pour over game hens. Cover casserole and bake at 325 degrees for 30 minutes. Take game hens out of casserole and stir chicken soup, wine, and sour cream into sauce in casserole. Add pepper to taste and return game hens to casserole. Bake in 350 degree oven uncovered for 15-20 minutes, or until heated thoroughly.

Doves

6-8   doves
1-2   tablespoons flour
4   tablespoons olive oil
2   tablespoons butter
2   cloves garlic, chopped
2   teaspoons chopped parsley
1½   cups Sebastiani Chardonnay or Sauvignon Blanc
    thyme, rosemary to taste
    salt, pepper to taste

Sprinkle doves with salt and pepper on all sides and in cavities. Dust lightly with flour and brown well in oil and butter. Add garlic, parsley, thyme, and rosemary, and brown slightly. Add hot wine and simmer, covered, until doves are tender, about 30 minutes, or more, if necessary.

Sometimes I vary this recipe by adding ½ chopped onion and ½ cup tomato sauce. This makes a great dish when served over polenta.

Roast Wild Duck

1   duck
      juice of 1 lemon
1   green onion, whole
1   stalk of tender celery with leaves
1   clove garlic, mashed
1   sprig parsley (optional)
¼   of an apple, whole
1   sprig thyme
2   tablespoons Heinz 57 Steak Sauce
      (optional)
      salt
      pepper

Rub duck with lemon juice on all sides. Salt and pepper generously on all sides and in cavity. Place remaining ingredients inside bird's cavity. Place on broiler pan and put into 500 degree oven. If cooking more than 1 duck at a time, do not put them too close together. Cook large ducks (mallards) 20-25 minutes; medium ducks (sprig) 15-18 minutes; small ducks (teals) 12-15 minutes. Ducks will be just slightly on the pink side, but not rare.

I have probably cooked more ducks than any one I know, but few cooks agree on how to serve roast wild duck. There is no doubt that a duck on the rare side is more tender and juicy than one that has been cooked well-done. However, there is no need to apologize if you don't like rare duck - just cook them a little longer. I do hope you have a self-cleaning oven, too.

Wild Duck Antoinette

1   duck
      garlic salt
      thyme, fresh or powdered
      salt
      pepper
1   pt. vegetable oil

If your duck is large, like a Mallard, Canvasback, or Sprig, cut into 6 parts. If your duck is smaller, cut into 4 pieces. Generously sprinkle garlic salt, thyme, salt and pepper over duck pieces, then dip into flour. Deep-fry ducks in a 10 inch frying pan in vegetable oil. Fry 10-15 minutes, depending on how you like your duck. If you use fresh thyme, add 2 or 3 sprigs after duck has been frying about 5 minutes and turn once. Serves 2.

The perfect accompaniment with duck prepared in this manner is a good green salad with olive oil and vinegar and a bottle of Gamay Beaujolais (guess whose?).

Roast Wild Goose

1   **wild goose, cleaned and dressed**
       juice of 1 lemon
       salt, pepper, garlic salt to taste
2   **green onions, whole**
1   **stalk celery (tender part with greens)**
1   **clove garlic, mashed**
1   **sprig rosemary or thyme**
4   **tablespoons oil**
½   **cup Sebastiani Pinot Noir or Barbera**
½   **cup August Sebastiani Country Chardonnay**

Rub goose with lemon juice; then sprinkle salt, pepper, and garlic salt on all sides and in cavity. Place onions, celery, garlic, and rosemary in cavity. Place in a deep Dutch oven along with oil. Roast, uncovered for 20 minutes at 400 degrees. Add heated wine and cover, reducing heat to 350 degrees. Cook until goose is tender when tested with a fork. May take anywhere from 2-2½ hours, depending on the age of the goose. Baste goose 2 or 3 times while baking. You may need to add more wine if there isn't enough juice. Serves 3-4 depending on the size of the goose.

Sebastiani Barbera goes well with this dish.

Stewed Rabbit

1-3   **lb. rabbit, cut into pieces**
2   **tablespoons olive oil**
2   **tablespoons butter**
1   **onion, chopped**
2   **stalks celery, chopped**
1   **small green pepper, chopped**
1   **clove garlic**
1   **8 oz. can tomato sauce**
1   **8 oz. can peeled tomatoes, chopped**
1   **sprig rosemary or ¼ teaspoon dry rosemary**
1   **cup August Sebastiani Chablis or Country Chardonnay**

In a Dutch oven or deep frying pan, heat butter and oil. Brown rabbit, adding salt and pepper on all sides. Remove rabbit and set aside. Brown onion, green pepper, and celery with a little more salt and pepper, adding garlic lastly. Add tomato sauce, tomatoes, rosemary, and wine. Cook slowly for 30 minutes, uncovered. Return rabbit to sauce. Cover and cook about 45 minutes until rabbit is tender. Serves 4.

Polenta serves as a good accompaniment to this dish. (see recipe in the Miscellaneous section of this book.)

Squabs in White Wine

6   squabs or small chickens
3   tablespoons olive oil
3   tablespoons butter
1½ cups Sebastiani Chardonnay
6   squab livers
2   chicken livers
8   shallots, finely choped
1   8 oz. can sliced button mushrooms
     salt, pepper to taste
     chopped parsley

In a shallow roasting pan, place birds that have been seasoned well with salt and pepper on all sides. Brown in 350 degree oven for 30 minutes. Pour heated wine over birds and cook 15 minutes longer. Add birds' livers, shallots, and mushrooms with their liquid. Cook for an additional 15 minutes until birds are tender. Transfer birds to a heated plate, pour pan juices over them, and sprinkle with chopped parsley. Serves 6-8.

Venison Heart

1   deer heart, cut into ¼ in. slices
3   tablespoons butter
3   tablespoons olive oil
     salt
     pepper
     flour

Season heart slices with salt and pepper, then dip into flour. Heat butter and oil in frying pan and fry 3-4 minutes on each side. Pour over pan juices before serving. Serves 4.

We accompany this dish with Sebastiani Zinfandel.

Venison Liver

1   lb. thinly-sliced venison liver
3   tablespoons butter
3   tablespoons olive oil
     salt
     pepper
     flour
2   teaspoons chopped parsley

Season liver slices with salt and pepper and dip into flour. Heat butter and oil in frying pan and saute liver slices quickly, 1-2 minutes on each side. Do not overcook liver as it gets tough. Pour over pan juices and sprinkle with chopped parsley before serving. Serves 4.

Venison Pot Roast

1   4-6 lb. venison pot roast
¼   cup wine vinegar
1   teaspoon salt
1   teaspoon pepper
1   teaspoon onion salt
1   teaspoon garlic salt
1   teaspoon celery salt
2   onions, chopped
2-3   cloves garlic, chopped
½   teaspoon thyme
½   teaspoon chopped basil
½   teaspoon paprika
1   pinch chopped red chili
1   can solid pack tomatoes, chopped
2   cups August Sebastiani Burgundy
     or Country Cabernet Sauvignon
2   teaspoons Worcestershire sauce

Saturate a cloth with vinegar; wring out and wipe meat thoroughly. Heat oil in heavy skillet or Dutch oven. Brown meat slowly on all sides; add salt, pepper, onion salt, garlic salt, and celery salt while browning meat. Then add onion and brown, stirring frequently. Add remaining ingredients, making sure wine is heated, cover and cook for 2½-3 hours.

Venison Scallopine

1½   lb. piece venison steak
     flour seasoned with salt and pepper
4   tablespoons olive oil
2   tablespoons butter
1   clove garlic, minced
     sprinkling of sage
     sprinkling of thyme
½   cup Sebastiani Chenin Blanc or
     August Sebastiani
     Country Chardonnay
½   cup water
     salt, pepper to taste

Slice venison into serving-size pieces and pound well. Coat pieces well with flour mixture. Heat oil and butter in frying pan, then add venison and brown on both sides. Add garlic and season to taste with salt and pepper. Sprinkle with sage and thyme. Pour over wine and water, then cover and bake at 350 degrees for 45 minutes to 1 hour until tender. Serves 4.

With this dish, we serve Sebastiani Cabernet Sauvignon.

Venison Stew

1½   lb. venison, cut into 1½ inch cubes
2   tablespoons flour
½   teaspoon salt
½   teaspoon pepper
½   teaspoon garlic salt
¼   cup oil
¼   cup butter
2   stalks celery, chopped
1   onion, chopped
2   cloves garlic, pressed
4   sprigs parsley, chopped
½   teaspoon thyme
½   teaspoon sage
1½   cups August Sebastiani Burgundy or Country Zinfandel
½   cup water

Coat venison in flour seasoned with salt, pepper, and garlic salt. Brown well in oil and butter, adding celery and onion. Add garlic and parsley and brown slightly. Add thyme and sage; then pour wine and water over all. Simmer, covered, over low heat or in a 325 degree oven for 1-1½ hours until meat is tender. Serves 6.

This stew is delightful served over rice or noodles and with a green salad, it makes a very nourishing dinner, and it is also very good made with either beef or veal. Serve with the Burgundy or Zinfandel left over from cooking.

Game Sauce

1   cube butter
4   tablespoons ketchup
    juice of 1 lemon
2   tablespoons Worcestershire
2   tablespoons Heinz 57 Steak Sauce
4   tablespoons Sebastiani Cabernet Sauvignon or Zinfandel

Melt butter in saucepan. Add remaining ingredients. Cook 10 minutes and serve. This sauce is excellent over wild duck or wild goose.

Venison or Beef Jerky

slices of venison or beef, ½ inch
     thick and 4 inches long
salt, pepper

Season meat slices with salt and pepper. Put into a pan and refrigerate over night. Pour off any liquid before stringing with heavy thread. Hang lines of meat in a wire mesh cage and place cage in direct sunlight for 4-5 days. At evening, place a canvas over the cage so that the meat does not absorb any moisture. Store in a tin covered with cheesecloth or paper. Keeps for several months.

Oven Cured Jerky

Follow above ingredients and instructions, except instead of outdoor curing, place meat on oven racks and put into oven at lowest possible temperature. Turn oven on for one hour and off for one hour, for about 12 hours, or until meat is dried.

Salads

Suggestions

1. When washing lettuce, squeeze the juice of 1 or 2 lemons into the water and also add about ½ teaspoon salt. The lemon juice adds to the crispness of the lettuce and the salt will drive out any insects hidden in the lettuce leaves.

2. If lettuce seems to be limp, add ice cubes to the water and allow lettuce to soak a few minutes.

3. After thorough washing, dry lettuce leaves thoroughly between towels or drain well in a salad basket.

4. Always chill lettuce after it is cleaned. Put in a cloth bag or other closed container in refrigerator to keep cold and crispy.

5. If you wish tomatoes to be added to a salad, prepare them separately and use them as garnish. If they are added along with the other ingredients, their juice will thin the dressing.

6. It is best to cut tomatoes in vertical slices because they bleed less this way.

7. A tastier tossed salad will result if several kinds of lettuce are used.

8. Always taste a tossed salad before serving. If it seems dull, add a little more vinegar or salt and pepper.

9. For molded salads, always rinse mold out with cold water before using. To unmold, dip mold in hot water, shake until loose, and unmold quickly.

10. Chill salad plates (bowls), especially if serving individual salads.

11. For a change of pace, try chilling the salad forks, too. You'll be amazed at the reactions you'll receive.

Apricot-Pistache Salad

2   3 oz. packages cream cheese
1   tablespoon cream
½   cup pistachio nuts, chopped fine
    pinch of salt (optional)
18   canned apricot halves
1   small head lettuce
½   cup French dressing
1   tablespoon bottled lime juice

Mash cream cheese with cream until smooth. Add nuts and salt. Form this mixture into 18 balls, ¾ inch in diameter. Arrange 3 apricot halves, round side down, on each of 6 individual beds of lettuce. Place a cheese ball in the center of each half and serve with French dressing mixed with lime juice. Serves 6.

Bean and Tuna Salad

1   can red kidney beans
½   red dry onion, chopped
1   6½ oz. can tuna
4   tablespoons oil
2   tablespoons finely chopped parsley
1   clove garlic, minced
    wine vinegar
    salt, pepper to taste

Drain and wash beans in a colander. Mix all ingredients in a bowl, adding salt and pepper to taste. Chill and serve. Serves 4-6.

This salad is great for barbeques during the summer months.

Bengal Salad

1   cup crab legs
1   cup shrimp
1½   cups onion, chopped fine
1   cup celery, diced
½   cup water chestnuts, sliced
1   13½ oz. can pineapple tidbits, drained
1½   cups pimiento, chopped
2   tablespoons currants
    juice of 1 lemon
4   tablespoons chutney
    salt to taste

Combine all ingredients in the order given and mix together well. Mix dressing ingredients and pour over the crab–shrimp mixture. Toss well. Serves 6.

Dressing:
1   cup mayonnaise
½   cup sour cream
½   teaspoon curry powder

This salad is marvelous for luncheon on a hot day. It can be made up the day before serving, if the crab and shrimp are withheld.

Caesar Salad

1 clove garlic
½-¾ cup olive oil or other salad oil
2 cups garlic croutons
2 large heads romaine lettuce
¾ teaspoon salt
generous gratings of black pepper
1½ teaspoons Worcestershire sauce
¼ teaspoon dry mustard
2 eggs, boiled 1½ minutes
juice of 1 lemon
6-8 anchovy filets, chopped fine
½ cup grated Parmesan cheese

Crush garlic and pour into ¼ cup oil; add croutons and set aside. Tear lettuce into large salad bowl, sprinkle salt and add pepper. Mix Worcestershire and mustard with remaining oil and pour over lettuce; tossing well. Break eggs into salad. Add lemon juice and toss thoroughly. Add anchovies and cheese and toss again. Add croutons, lastly, toss gently, and serve immediately. Serves 12.

Celery Victor

1 can hearts of celery, well-drained
1 cup well-seasoned French dressing
1 small head lettuce, shredded
coarsely ground black pepper
8 anchovy filets
2 grated hard-boiled eggs
1 avocado, sliced (optional)
1 tomato, sliced (optional)

Pour French dressing over celery hearts and let chill several hours. Drain off most of dressing and place celery on shredded lettuce. Sprinkle with pepper, place anchovies on top, and cover with grated egg. Avocado and tomato may be used for extra garnish if so desired. Serves 4.

Crab Salad

1 can tomato soup - 10 ¾ oz
2 small packages cream cheese
3 tablespoons unflavored gelatin
softened in ½ cup cold water
¾ teaspoon salt
½ green pepper, chopped fine
1 cup celery, chopped fine
1 small onion, chopped fine
1 large can crabmeat
1 cup mayonnaise

Heat soup; add cream cheese and gelatin. Blend well. Add salt, pepper, celery, onion, crab and mayonnaise to mixture. Pour into mold, chill, and serve cold. Serves 6.

Cranberry Salad

2   packages cherry gelatin
2   cups boiling water
1½   cups sugar
     juice of 1 orange
     juice of 1 lemon
1   package raw cranberries, chopped
1   cup nuts, chopped
1   red apple, unpeeled and chopped
2   cups celery, chopped

Dissolve gelatin in boiling water. Add sugar, orange juice, and lemon juice. Then add cranberries, nuts, apple, and celery, mixing well. Chill in large mold or individual molds. Serves 8-10.

Fruit Cocktail with Wine

2   cans fruit cocktail, any size
1   can mandarin oranges
     fresh fruit on hand, e.g., apples, bananas, peaches
1   sprig mint
¼   cup Sebastiani Gewurztraminer or August Sebastiani Country Chenin Blanc

Mix all ingredients together and chill well. Serve as a fruit cup for a first course instead of a salad. Serves 6-8.

Green Goddess Salad

5   anchovy filets (anchovy paste may be used instead)
2   green onions, chopped
¼   cup minced parsley
1   clove garlic
1   large head lettuce
1½   cups mayonnaise
2   tablespoons tarragon vinegar
1   lb. cooked lobster, shrimp, or crab meat (optional)

Chop together anchovies and onions until finely minced; then add parsley. Rub a salad bowl with garlic and cut lettuce into bite-sized pieces, then place into bowl. Stir mayonnaise and vinegar into the anchovy mixture and mix well. Pour over lettuce, tossing thoroughly. Spoon onto individual salad plates and garnish with shellfish if desired. Serves 6.

Gelatin Ribbon Salad

2   packages cherry gelatin
4-5   cups boiling water
1   No. 2½ can fruit salad, save juice
1   package lemon gelatin
1   cup mayonnaise
2   small packages cream cheese

Dissolve 1 package cherry gelatin in 2 cups water. Put in bottom of pan with drained fruit salad and set until firm. Dissolve lemon gelatin in juice from fruit and add enough boiling water to make 2 cups. Blend mayonnaise and cheese; add to lemon gelatin when it begins to congeal. Spread on top of firm cherry gelatin. Dissolve other package of cherry gelatin in 2 cups boiling water and place on top of lemon gelatin mixture. Chill until firm. Serves 8.

Marinated Beans Salad

1   303 size can green beans, undrained
1   303 size can wax beans, undrained
1   303 size can kidney beans, drained and rinsed
1   303 size can garbanzo beans, drained
1   303 size can okra, drained
½   cup sugar
⅔   cup apple cider vinegar
⅔   cup oil
1   teaspoon salt
½   teaspoon pepper
½   cup green peppers, chopped fine
2   medium onions, cut in thin rings

Mix all beans with sugar, vinegar, oil, salt, and pepper. Then add green peppers and onions. Chill. Serves 12-15.

Mary Ann's Shrimp Salad

1   head Romaine lettuce
1   4½ oz. can shrimp, well-drained
1   cup mayonnaise
1   tablespoon white vinegar
1   teaspoon dry mustard
½   teaspoon beau monde seasoning
½   teaspoon lemon celery seasoning
3   tablespoons ketchup
2   hard-boiled eggs, chopped
1   sweet pickle, chopped fine (optional)
     salt, white pepper, garlic salt to taste

Trim both ends from head of lettuce. Leaving head intact, cut into quarters length-wise and place each quarter on an individual plate. Combine remaining ingredients and pour over each quarter of lettuce. Serves 4.

Mixed Green Salad

1   head romaine lettuce, heart only
1   head endive
1   head butter lettuce
2-10 radishes, sliced thin
3   stalks celery heart, chopped
2   green onions, chopped
     grated Parmesan cheese (optional)

Dressing:
2   anchovy filets
1   tablespoon wine vinegar
3   tablespoons olive oil
¼   teaspoon dry mustard
1   clove garlic, mashed
     salt, pepper to taste

Wash and clean all lettuce and let drain thoroughly. Break into bite-size pieces and mix with radishes, celery, and onion in salad bowl. Chop anchovies and combine with remaining ingredients. Beat with a fork until dressing thickens. Pour over salad and toss lightly. Sprinkle with Parmesan cheese if desired. Serves 8-10.

There are many ways to vary a mixed green salad. Here are some suggestions: 1) add onion rings; 2) add sliced raw mushrooms; 3) add cubes of avocadoes; 4) add peeled, sliced cucumbers; 5) add cooked crab or shrimp; 6) add strips of cold chicken, turkey, ham, or shredded tuna.

Orange Gelatin Salad

2   packages orange gelatin
1   cup boiling water
2   cans mandarin oranges, save juice
1   pint orange sherbet
1   cup sour cream
1   13 oz. can pineapple tidbits

Dissolve gelatin in boiling water. Add juice from oranges and chill until mixture begins to jell. Add sherbet and sour cream and beat until frothy. Add pineapple and oranges. Pour into mold and chill overnight. Serves 12.

Orange-Lemon Pudding Salad

2   packages orange gelatin
2½   cups boiling water
1   6 oz. can frozen orange juice, thawed
1   can mandarin oranges, drained
1   cup crushed pineapple, drained
1   package lemon pie filling
½   pint whipping cream

Add boiling water to gelatin. Then add orange juice, oranges and pineapple. Set until firm. Mix pie filling and cook as directed on package. Let cool. Whip cream and fold into the cooled lemon filling. Spread this over the orange gelatin mixture. Serves 8-10.

Pineapple-Cottage Cheese Salad

1   package lime gelatin
1   package lemon gelatin
2   cups boiling water
1   cup Pet milk
1   pt. cottage cheese, small curd
1   No. 2 can crushed pineapple
1   cup chopped nuts (walnuts or almonds)
1   tablespoon horseradish (optional)
1   cup mayonnaise

Mix lime gelatin and lemon gelatin together; add water and stir until gelatin is dissolved. Add milk, cottage cheese, pineapple, nuts, and horseradish to gelatin mixture and blend well. Finally, add mayonnaise and pour entire mixture into a mold. (A 13 x 8 rectangular baking dish works fine.) Chill and serve. Serves 8-10.

Potato Salad

4   or 5 medium potatoes
4   or 5 tablespoons white vinegar
3   hard-boiled eggs, chopped
1/2   chopped onion
4   stalks celery, chopped very fine
1/2   cup parsley, chopped
1   small pimento, chopped
    salt, pepper, garlic salt to taste
1   cup mayonnaise
1   teaspoon dry mustard
    paprika
8   olives
    few sprigs parsley

Boil potatoes with skins on in uncovered pot until tender, making sure all potatoes are covered with water. Drain, peel, and slice potatoes, then marinate them well with vinegar. Add eggs, onion, celery, parsley, pimiento, and seasonings with mayonnaise and mustard. Fold gently into potatoes and stir as little as possible. (Additional mayonnaise may be added as needed.) Sprinkle with paprika; garnish with olives and parsley sprigs. Serves 10.

Raw Spinach Salad

1/2   lb. raw spinach
1/4   cup green pepper, chopped
1/2   cup sweet onion rings
1 1/2   tablespoons lemon juice
1 1/2   tablespoons salad oil
1/4   teaspoon tarragon
1/2   teaspoon salt
1/8   teaspoon pepper
2   hard-boiled eggs, sliced
6   anchovy filets

Wash spinach and drain on paper towels to absorb excess water. Tear or cut leaves into bite-size pieces and put in a salad bowl. Add green pepper, onion rings, lemon juice, oil, tarragon, salt and pepper. Toss lightly. Garnish with egg slices and anchovies. Serves 6-8.

Ribbon Salad

1 large package lime gelatin
5 cups hot water
1 small package lemon gelatin
½ cup miniature marshmallows
1 20 oz. can crushed pineapple with juice
1 8 oz. package cream cheese
1 cup mayonnaise
½ pt. whipped cream
1 large package cherry gelatin
2 cups cold water

Dissolve lime gelatin in 2 cups hot water; pour into bottom of 14" x 10½" pan and chill until firm. Dissolve lemon gelatin in 1 cup hot water on top of double boiler. Add marshmallows and stir to melt. Remove from heat and add crushed pineapple with juice. Then add cream cheese and blend well. Fold in mayonnaise and whipped cream. Pour over lime gelatin and chill until set. Dissolve cherry gelatin in 2 cups hot water and add 2 cups cold water. Pour over layers of lime and lemon gelatin and chill until firm. Serves 16.

Sliced Tomatoes with Basil

3 tomatoes
10 - 12 leaves fresh basil
1 tablespoon olive oil
1 tablespoon wine vinegar
   salt, pepper, garlic salt to taste
   red onion rings (optional)

Place tomato slices in over-lapping manner on a platter. Garnish with basil. Sprinkle with oil, vinegar, and seasonings. Add onion rings if desired. Serves 6-8.

The essential ingredient in this recipe is the fresh basil. If you have none on hand, then skip the recipe. If desired, the basil and onions can be chopped.

Tomatoes Stuffed with Cucumbers

6 ripe tomatoes
2 cucumbers
   salt, pepper to taste
   several lettuce leaves

Dressing:
½ cup sour cream
1 tablespoon lemon juice
1 tablespoon vinegar
½ teaspoon salt
⅛ teaspoon white pepper
½ teaspoon prepared mustard
2 teaspoons chopped parsley

Scald tomatoes so that skins can be easily removed. Cut a slice from the top of each peeled tomato and with a small spoon, scoop out the centers. Place on lettuce beds. Peel cucumbers, dice, and season with salt and pepper. Mix dressing by adding all ingredients to the sour cream and blending well. Add cucumbers to dressing mix and stir well. Fill tomato cups with cucumber mixture and sprinkle each cup with parsley. Serves 6.

Tomatoes Stuffed with Fish

4 medium tomatoes, peeled
1 cup shrimp, crab, or tuna
1 cup finely chopped tender celery
    stalks and leaves
2-3 green onions, chopped fine
1 teaspoon white vinegar
¼ teaspoon salt
⅛ teaspoon pepper
¼ cup mayonnaise
2 teaspoons lemon juice
    beau monde seasoning
    salt
    white pepper
    several lettuce leaves
    paprika
    parsley sprigs

Quarter peeled tomatoes, but do not cut entirely through. Add fish to celery and onion and mix well. Then add vinegar, salt, pepper, mayonnaise and lemon juice. Sprinkle tomatoes with beau monde seasoning, salt, and white pepper and place on bed of lettuce leaves. Spoon fish mixture over tomatoes, dot with mayonnaise, sprinkle with paprika, and top with a sprig of parsley. Serves 4.

To peel tomatoes easily, dip into boiling water 10-15 seconds, then remove and peel. If peel does not come off easily, dip into water a few seconds more, then peel.

Sour Cream Fruit Salad

1 pint sour cream
1 can mandarin oranges
1 can pineapple tidbits
1 cup shredded coconut
¾ package miniature marshmallows

Combine all ingredients together and chill. If left to stand overnight, the flavor will be improved greatly. Serves 6.

Tuna Salad

1 head romaine lettuce
1 red onion, sliced or chopped
1 small clove garlic, pressed
1 small can tuna, undrained
    vinegar, salt, pepper to taste

Break lettuce leaves into bite-size pieces. Add remaining ingredients and toss lightly. Season to taste. Serves 6. Additional oil may be added if desired.

Waldorf Salad

1 cup celery, diced
1 cup diced apples, red and unpeeled
½ cup walnut or pecan meats
¾ cup mayonnaise
   several lettuce leaves

Combine celery, apples, nuts and mayonnaise together, mixing well. Serve on a bed of lettuce leaves. Serves 4-6.

Watercress Salad

2 large bunches watercress
3 tablespoons olive oil
2 tablespoons wine vinegar
   juice of ½ lemon
   salt, pepper to taste
   few sliced water chestnuts (optional)

Wash watercress and dry leaves thoroughly. Place leaves in salad bowl, sprinkle with salt and pepper, and chill well. Just prior to serving, mix oil, vinegar, and lemon juice together and sprinkle over watercress. Add water chestnuts and toss lightly. Serves 6-8.

Basic French Dressing

¾ teaspoon salt
½ teaspoon black pepper
½ teaspoon dry mustard
1 clove garlic,
½ cup wine vinegar
1½ cups olive oil

Add salt, pepper, mustard, and garlic to vinegar. Stir well with a fork, then add oil. Beat well until dressing thickens. Remove garlic before using. Makes about 2 cups.

This dressing can be easily made up ahead of time and refrigerated, but be sure to remove the clove of garlic after 24 hours. Also, if dressing is refrigerated, let stand at room temperature for half an hour before serving so that the ingredients have a chance to blend.

Watercress Dressing

½ cup watercress leaves
1 clove garlic, minced
1 cup mayonnaise
2 teaspoons lemon juice
   salt, pepper to taste

Chop watercress and garlic together until very fine. Stir into mayonnaise and lemon juice. Season to taste with salt and pepper. Chill. Serve over wedges of head lettuce. Makes about 1½ cups.

Casseroles

Easy Baked Beans

2	slices bacon, cut into 1 in. pieces
½	onion, chopped
1	clove garlic, chopped or pressed
1	16 oz. can solid pack tomatoes (mashed)
⅔	cup August Sebastiani Chablis or Country Chardonnay
1	27 oz. can red kidney beans, drained salt, pepper to taste

Fry bacon, not too crisp, and pour out excess grease from pan. Sauté onion with bacon, adding salt and pepper to taste. Then add garlic, tomatoes, and wine. Cover and simmer for 30 minutes. Add beans and transfer to a casserole dish. Bake uncovered in 350 degree oven for 30 minutes. Serves 4.

Bean Mushroom Casserole

1	No.2 can french style green beans
1	can cream of mushroom soup, undiluted
1	package frozen french fried onions

Place the beans in a buttered casserole. Spoon soup over beans, making a smooth layer. Place onions evenly over this. Bake in a moderately hot oven (320 degrees) for 30-40 minutes, until hot and bubbly. Serve 4-6.

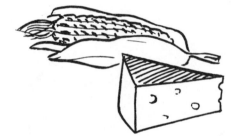

Cheese Corn Soufflé

3	eggs, separated
½	teaspoon salt
1	8¾ oz. can cream style corn
1	tablespoon chopped green onions
¼	cup August Sebastiani Country French Colombard or Country Fumé Blanc
1	tablespoon quick-cooking tapioca dash tabasco sauce
1	cup process American cheese, shredded

Add salt to egg whites and beat until stiff. With same beater, beat yolks slightly. Combine corn, onion, wine, tapioca, and tabasco sauce in a small saucepan. Heat to boiling, stirring constantly. Remove from heat and stir into beaten egg yolks. Add cheese and mix well; then fold in egg whites. Turn into a 1 qt. baking dish and bake at 350 degrees for 45 minutes until well-puffed and browned on top. Serve at once from baking dish. Serves 4-6.

Chicken Casserole

3   cups cooked boneless chicken, cut
      in pieces
1   10½ oz, can cream of chicken soup,
      undiluted
1   tablespoon lemon juice
¾   cup mayonnaise
1   cup diced celery
2   teaspoons minced onion
½   cup chopped walnuts
½   teaspoon salt
¼   teaspoon pepper
3   hard-boiled eggs, sliced thin
4   tablespoons August Sebastiani Chablis
      or Country Chenin Blanc
4   tablespoons cooked rice
1   cup sliced mushrooms
      few dashes Worcestershire sauce
2   cups crushed potato chips
      paprika

Mix all ingredients, except potato chips and paprika, together in a large bowl. Pour into a greased casserole dish. Sprinkle with paprika and top with potato chips. Bake 20 minutes at 450 degrees. Serves 8.

Confetti Casserole

2   cups cooked elbow macaroni
1   lb. ground round
1   onion, chopped
⅛   teaspoon oregano
1   clove garlic, pressed
1   can vegetable soup, undiluted
1   medium can of tomatoes, chopped
½   cup grated Parmesan cheese

Cook macaroni as directed on package. Brown meat with onion, spices, and garlic. Mix macaroni, meat mixture, soup, and tomatoes together. Put in baking dish and cover with cheese. Bake ½ hour in 350 degree oven. Serves 6-8.

Mamie's Hash

1   onion, chopped
1 or 2 slices bacon, cut into small
         pieces
2   cups cooked ham or corned beef,
        ground or chopped
1½   cups raw potatoes, cubed
1   clove garlic
⅔   cup tomato sauce
4   tablespoons August Sebastiani Chablis
        or Country French Colombard
        salt, pepper to taste

Saute onion with bacon, but do not overcook. Add remaining ingredients and pour into a greased casserole dish. Bake 45 minutes at 350 degrees.

Mushroom Torta

3	cups boiled mushrooms, drained and chopped
¼	cup chopped parsley
4	cloves garlic, pressed
3	medium onions, chopped
2	teaspoons basil
1	teaspoon oregano
2	teaspoons marjoram
½	teaspoon sage
¼	cup olive oil
6	whole eggs
2	teaspoons salt
½	teaspoon pepper
½	teaspoon paprika
1½	cups grated Parmesan cheese
¾	cup bread crumbs

Sauté mushrooms, parsley, garlic, onions, and spices in oil until onion is transparent. Remove from stove and set aside. Whip eggs with fork in large bowl with salt, pepper, and paprika. Add mushroom mixture and stir so that egg does not cook. Add cheese and stir; then add bread crumbs, a small amount at a time, until mixture is the consistency of dressing. Grease a baking dish and sprinkle with bread crumbs, shaking out excess. Pour mixture into dish, but do not pack. Sprinkle a little oil and bread crumbs on top. Bake at 350 degrees for ½ hour until light brown. Do not overbake. Serves 6-8.

This torta can be made ahead of serving time and refrigerated until ready for baking. Let stand at room temperature 30 minutes before placing into oven. Can be served hot or cold.

Plantation Eggs

16	hard-boiled eggs, chopped
4	tablespoons butter
6	tablespoons flour
4	cups milk
6	tablespoons vinegar
4	tablespoons dry mustard
2	teaspoons salt
4	tablespoons mayonnaise
2	packages cheddar cheese, (grated)
	slices of Canadian bacon

Mix chopped eggs in a baking dish. Make cream sauce by combining butter, flour, and milk. Add vinegar, mustard, and salt, stirring well. Cook until thick and cool. Add mayonnaise and blend well. Pour over eggs and cover with cheese. Bake in 350 degree oven for 25 minutes, making sure not to overbake. Serve over slices of fried Canadian bacon. Serves 10-12.

Shellfish Casserole

1   cup vegetable or tomato juice
1   cup mayonnaise
1   can crabmeat or 1 cup fresh crab
1   can shrimp or 1 cup fresh shrimp
2   cups cooked rice
⅓   cup chopped green pepper
2   tablespoons butter
1   cup bread crumbs
½   cup slivered almonds
     salt, pepper to taste

Combine juice and mayonnaise and mix well. Stir in crab, shrimp, rice, and green pepper. Salt and pepper to taste. Mix until ingredients are well-distributed. Pour into a greased 2 quart casserole. In a small pan, melt butter and add bread crumbs and almonds. Mix with fork until all crumbs are coated with butter. Pour over casserole. Bake at 375 degrees for about ½ hour. Serves 8.

Spinach Casserole

2   Packages frozen chopped spinach
1   package fresh mushrooms, sliced
1   small onion, chopped
½   cup celery, chopped
1   can cream of mushroom soup, undiluted

Defrost and break apart spinach. Sauté mushrooms with onion and celery until all are tender. Combine with spinach and soup in a greased casserole. Bake at 375 degrees for 30 minutes. Serves 8.

Tamale Pie

1   onion, chopped
2   cloves garlic, chopped
2   tablespoons olive oil
2   tablespoons butter
1   lb. ground round
½   lb. ground pork
1   can pitted olives with liquid
1   can creamed corn
1   8 oz. can tomato sauce
¾   cup polenta
1   green pepper, chopped
¾   cup milk
2-3   eggs, slightly beaten
2-3   tablespoons chili powder
1   cup water
     salt, pepper to taste

Sauté onion and garlic lightly in oil and butter. Add meats, season with salt and pepper, and keep stirring. Add corn, olives, 4-5 tablespoons olive liquid, and tomato sauce. Stir well, then add polenta and cook together. Add green pepper and salt and pepper to taste once again. Add milk, eggs, chili powder and water, mix well. Place in a greased casserole dish and bake 30-40 minutes at 300 degrees.

Desserts + Cookies

Suggestions

1. To assure proper baking, be sure that your oven thermostat is accurate. To test, simply place an oven thermometer inside oven and check its temperature with that shown on the oven control.

2. Always read recipe thoroughly and make sure you have all ingredients in their sufficient amounts on hand.

3. Butter gives all desserts a better flavor and texture more than any other shortening. Pure vanilla is also preferred to imitation vanilla.

4. If a piece of egg shell drops into a broken egg in a bowl, it can easily be removed by using a piece of eggshell as a spoon. And when separating eggs, if a bit of yolk is in the whites, use this same method to get the yolk out.

5. Be accurate in measuring all ingredients and be sure to use only the specified amount of each.

6. Check that you have the proper size baking tins on hand and that they are always clean.

7. Strawberries are delicious when served with any wine or champagne. For an extra touch, I like to rinse the berries, after they are stemmed, with a white dinner wine, instead of washing them with water. When this is done, no watery flavor results in the berries.

8. If you like to make a great many cookies for gifts, especially at Christmas time, you will save time and fuel if you buy two or more racks for your oven. You will thus be able to bake four pans of cookies at a time and cut your baking time in half.

9. When baking a great many cookies, use more pans than racks in oven so that rotation is possible. Take the pan on the top rack out of the oven, move all other pans up one rack, and place a new pan in on the bottom rack. This helps eliminate burning the bottom of the cookies and keeps them from being too brown on top.

Apricot Bars

1½ cups flour
1 teaspoon baking powder
1 cup brown sugar
1½ cups quick oats
¾ cup butter
1 pint apricot jam

Mix flour, baking powder, sugar, and oats together. Mix well, then cut in butter until texture of pie crust. In greased pan (8x13), put 2/3 of the mixture and pat firm. Spread jam over this. Put the rest of the mixture on top. Bake at 325 degrees for 45 minutes. Cool and cut into squares, lifting out with a spatula.

Bon Bons

2 egg whites
  Pinch cream of tartar
1 cup sugar
½ teaspoon vanilla
¼ teaspoon green food coloring
1 6 oz. package mint-flavored chocolate chips

Preheat oven to 350 degrees. Stiffly beat egg whites with cream of tartar. Slowly add sugar, vanilla and food coloring. Fold in chocolate chips. (Add more food coloring if necessary.) Drop by tablespoonfuls onto foil covered cookie sheets. Turn off oven, place cookie sheets in, and leave overnight. Remove the next morning. DO NOT PEEK! Makes about 4 dozen.

Lace Curtain Cookies

1 cup flour
1 cup chopped nuts
½ cup corn syrup
½ cup shortening
⅓ cup brown sugar

Blend flour and nuts and set aside. Bring corn syrup, shortening, and sugar to boil over medium heat, stirring constantly. Remove from heat and gradually stir in flour and nuts. Drop by level teaspoonfuls on lightly greased baking sheet about 3 inches apart. Bake in 375 degree oven for 5 minutes. Let stand 5 minutes before removing from baking sheet. Makes about 3 dozen.

Aunt Mary's Italian Biscotti

½   cup butter
¾   cup sugar
3   eggs
½   teaspoon vanilla
3   cups flour
3   teaspoons baking powder
½   teaspoon salt
1   tablespoon anise seed
2   tablespoons grated lemon peel
2   tablespoons grated orange peel
1   cup chopped almonds

Cream butter and sugar, then add eggs one at a time, beating well after each addition. Add vanilla. Sift together flour, baking powder, and salt and add slowly to creamed mixture. Stir in lemon and orange peels, anise seed, and nuts and blend well. Divide dough into 3 parts and shape each part into a long roll about 1½ inches in diameter. Place rolls onto cookie sheet several inches apart and flatten rolls somewhat. Bake at 350 degrees for 15 minutes. Then remove from oven and slice rolls crosswise ¾ inches thick. Lay cut side down on cookie sheet, return to oven and bake an additional 15 minutes. Makes about 4 dozen.

This recipe makes a biscotti which is not very sweet in the traditional manner of Italian baking. If you prefer things sweet, increase the amount of sugar to 1 full cup. For something different, try dunking these biscotti in a glass of Sebastiani Gamay Beaujolais.

Brown Sugar Apple Crisp

6 apples, peeled and sliced
6 tablespoons water
½ cup sugar
1 teaspoon cinnamon
1 teaspoon nutmeg
1 cup brown sugar
½ stick butter
1 cup flour
½ pt. whipping cream

Place apples in buttered baking dish. Cover with water, sugar, and spices. Work butter, brown sugar, and flour together until the consistency of cornmeal. Crumble this mixture on top of apples and sprinkle with more spices as desired. Bake 30 minutes at 350 degrees. Serve with whipped cream.

Burned Peaches

6 canned peach halves, save syrup
½ cup sugar
2 tablespoons brown sugar
2 tablespoons cinnamon
2 tablespoons lemon juice
6 teaspoons currant jelly
6 teaspoons brandy

Take juice from peaches and add sugar and brown sugar. Boil for 25 minutes or until thick. Place peach halves in pyrex baking dish. Sprinkle with cinnamon and lemon juice. Place 1 teaspoon jelly in center of each half. Pour peach juice around and bake for 20 minutes at 350 degrees. Pour over brandy just before serving, set flame, and burn. Serves 6.

Peaches in Wine Sauce

4 large fresh peaches
¾ cup sugar
2 cups water
1 teaspoon vanilla
2 egg yolks
¼ teaspoon salt
¾ cup sifted powdered sugar
⅓ cup Sebastiani Gewurztraminer or August Sebastiani Country Chenin Blanc
1 cup whipping cream
   nutmeg

Peel, pit, and halve peaches. Boil sugar and water. Add peaches. Simmer 5-10 minutes until peaches are tender. Add vanilla and chill until ready to serve. Beat egg yolks and salt until thick and lemon-colored. Add sugar gradually and beat until thick. Add wine. Whip cream and fold into egg yolk mixture. Spoon over the peaches and sprinkle with nutmeg. Serves 8.

Canned peaches may be used instead of fresh peaches.

Brandy Balls

2 tablespoons cocoa
1 cup powdered sugar
⅓ cup brandy
2 tablespoons corn syrup
2 cups vanilla wafers, finely crushed
1 cup chopped walnuts or pecans
   granulated sugar

Sift together cocoa and sugar. Combine and stir in brandy and corn syrup. Combine crushed wafers and nuts. Add chocolate mixture and mix well. Form into 1 inch balls and roll in sugar. Let sit in covered container several days. Makes about 4 dozen.

Brandy Pineapples

4 macaroons
1 20 oz. can pineapple chunks, save juice
4 jiggers brandy
½ cup slivered almonds

Place 1 macaroon at bottom of each of 4 sherbet glasses. Spoon pineapple chunks into each glass and cover with 1 tablespoon pineapple juice. Pour 1 jigger brandy into each glass and top with slivered almonds. Chill for at least 2 hours before serving. Serves 4.

For an original twist, make your own macaroons following the recipe in this book. They're simple, quick and very delicious.

Chess Tarts

pastry for 1 pie crust (see recipe in this book)
1 scant cup sugar
½ cup butter, softened
1 or 2 eggs
½ cup currants
1 cup chopped nuts
1 cup shredded coconut
1 teaspoon vanilla
   glazed fruits (optional)

Line small muffin tins with pastry. With electric mixer, cream sugar and butter. Add remaining ingredients and mix well. Fill pastry shells and bake at 375 degrees for 20 minutes. Makes about 3 dozen.

Bugie (Sweet Pastry)

2 cups flour
2-3 eggs
2 tablespoons rum
  powdered sugar
⅛ teaspoon salt
  oil for deep frying

Place flour in a bowl and make a well in the center. Add eggs, rum, 1 tablespoon sugar, and salt. Mix ingredients until well-blended and dough can be gathered into a rough ball. Sprinkle a little flour on a board or pastry cloth and knead for 10 minutes until dough is smooth and shiny. Refrigerate for 1 hour. Heat 3-4 inches oil in a deep fryer or deep, heavy saucepan. Roll out chilled dough, about ¼ at a time, until paper thin. Cut with a sharp knife into strips 6 inches long and ½ inch wide. Tie strips into loose knots and deep fry them, 4 or 5 at a time, for 1-2 minutes until they are delicately brown. With a strainer spoon, transfer bugie to paper towels to drain. Repeat procedure until all dough has been used. Just before serving, sprinkle with powdered sugar.

Panettone

2 cubes butter, softened
1½ cups sugar
4 eggs
1 cup milk
1 tablespoon vanilla
1 tablespoon brandy
1 tablespoon rum
1 tablespoon anise (optional)
1 tablespoon grated lemon peel
4 cups flour
4 teaspoons baking powder
1 teaspoon salt
1 cup raisins
½ cup citron, chopped
½ cup glazed cherries, chopped
½ cup pine nuts

Cream butter and sugar; then add eggs one at a time, beating well after each addition. Add milk, vanilla, brandy, rum, and anise and blend well. Sift flour, baking powder, and salt together and gradually add to creamed mixture. Fold in raisins, citron, cherries, and nuts until well-blended. Pour into a greased and floured 9-inch angel food pan and bake at 350 degrees for about 1 hour or until panettone is done when tested with a toothpick.

Crêpes Suzettes

6   eggs
1½   cups sifted flour
1¾   cups milk
½   teaspoon salt
1½   tablespoons sugar
½   cube butter, melted

Sauce:

       juice from 2 oranges
       few drops lemon juice
½   cup brandy
       granulated sugar

Beat eggs, flour, milk, salt, and sugar together. After batter is well-blended, pour in butter and blend well. Let batter stand at least 30 minutes before using. If it becomes too thick on standing, add a teaspoon of water or milk. Drop 2 tablespoons of batter into a well-buttered 6 inch skillet and cook over moderate heat. Fold the thin cake twice after removing from pan.

Sauce: Extract juice from oranges and set aside. Grind oranges and add to orange juice. Add lemon juice and ¼ cup brandy. Pour sauce over crêpes and sprinkle with granulated sugar. Just before serving, pour remaining brandy, heated, over crêpes. Ignite and serve flaming. Serves 10.

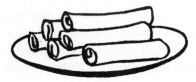

Gingerbread

½   cup butter
1½   cups brown sugar, firmly packed
2¼   cups dark molasses
10   cups flour
1½   teaspoons allspice
1½   teaspoons cinnamon
2½   teaspoons ginger
1½   teaspoons salt
1   cup cold water
1   tablespoon baking soda

Cream butter and sugar together until light and fluffy. Stir in molasses. Sift flour with spices and salt and add to creamed mixture alternately with ¾ cup water. Dissolve soda in remaining water and stir soda into dough. Chill before rolling out and cutting into whatever shapes you desire. Bake 20 minutes in 325 degree oven and cool. Decorate as you please.

It has long been a tradition in our home to have a gingerbread party every year at Christmas time. Even though some "children" are grown and married, they return to participate along with the grandchildren. This recipe yields quite a large amount of dough, so there is plenty for each child to be creative in his decorating. Gingerbread freezes quite well and we keep some gingerbread men in the freezer and pass them out to children when they come to visit.

Gelatin and Ice Cream

1   package strawberry gelatin
1¼   cups hot water
1   quart vanilla ice cream
½   pint whipping cream
      fresh strawberries (8)

Mix gelatin with hot water and chill, but do not let thicken. Cut ice cream into pieces and with rotary beater, add to gelatin, beating well until all ingredients are combined and smooth. Pour into individual sherbet glasses and chill until firm. Top with whipped cream and a strawberry. Serves 8.

This dessert can also be made with other flavors of gelatin, e.g., orange, raspberry, cherry, etc. The mixture may be poured into a baked pie shell and chilled for a different type of pie entirely.

Strawberry Shortcake

2½   cups Bisquick
3   tablespoons butter
3   tablespoons sugar
½   cup half and half cream
2   baskets strawberries
½   Pint whipping cream

Mix Bisquick, butter, sugar, and cream together, forming a soft dough. Knead 8-10 times on a lightly-floured board and roll ½ inch thick. Cut with a floured 3 inch cutter and bake on ungreased baking sheet in 450 degree oven for 10 minutes. Wash, hull and halve berries. Add desired amount of sugar to sweeten. Split warm shortcakes in two and spoon berries between and over layers. Top with whipped cream. Serves 6.

Baked Apples

4   apples, peeled
1   cup Sebastiani Gamay Beaujolais
      or Zinfandel
⅔   cup sugar
¼   cup cinnamon red hots (optional)
1   tablespoon lemon juice
4   teaspoons sour cream

Mix together wine, sugar, red hots, and lemon juice. Pour over apples and bake at 350 degrees for 50 minutes. Serve with a teaspoon of sour cream over each apple. Serves 4.

Chopped nuts may also be added to the center of apples before baking, if so desired.

Macaroons

3 egg whites
1 8 oz. can almond paste
1 cup sugar

Beat egg whites. Cut almond paste into small pieces and add to egg whites along with sugar. Mix until smooth and there are no lumps. Drop by rounded teaspoonfuls onto brown paper placed on top of cookie sheet. Bake in 325 degree oven for about 30 minutes. Allow to cool, then wet back of paper to remove macaroons easily. Makes about 3 dozen.

Meringue Cookies

3 egg whites
1½ cups sugar
3 teaspoons baking powder
    tiny colored candies

Beat egg whites until stiff. Add 2/3 of the sugar gradually. Add remaining sugar with baking powder. Put through pastry decorating tube and bake on brown paper at 350 degrees for 6 minutes. Top with tiny candies. Makes about 3 dozen.

Persimmon Cookies

½ cup shortening
1 cup sugar
1 egg
1 cup persimmon pulp
½ teaspoon cinnamon
½ teaspoon nutmeg
½ teaspoon cloves
½ teaspoon salt
½ teaspoon baking soda
2 cups flour
1 cup raisins
1 cup chopped nuts

Cream shortening and add sugar slowly. Then add egg and beat well. Add persimmon pulp, spices, salt, soda, and flour. Fold in raisins and nuts. Drop by teaspoonfuls onto greased cookie sheet. Bake in 350 degree oven for 10-15 minutes. Makes about 3 dozen.

Macaroon Trifle

¼   **lb. almond macaroons**
¼   **lb. ladyfingers**
½   **cup raspberry jam**
     custard sauce (below)
¼   **cup Sebastiani Johannisberg Riesling or August Sebastiani Country Chenin Blanc**
¼   **cup brandy**
     maraschino cherries
½   **pt. whipping cream**

Custard sauce:
2   **tablespoons cornstarch**
2   **cups milk**
3   **tablespoons sugar**
3   **egg yolks**
3   **tablespoons water**

Break macaroons and ladyfingers in two and mix together. Line a small bowl (about 6 cup size) with part of the jam. Add part of the cakes to lining of the bowl. Spread with remaining jam.

Make custard sauce by blending cornstarch with ½ cup cold milk. Heat remaining milk in double boiler, then stir in cornstarch mixture. Beat together sugar, egg yolks, and water. Add hot milk, stirring constantly. Cook 5-10 minutes to a thin custard consistency. Let cool. Add wine and brandy to cooled custard sauce and whip all three together. Add custard sauce to the remainder of the cakes and fill the bowl. Cover and refrigerate overnight. Just before serving, decorate with cherries and whipped cream.

Orange Sherry Cream

½   **cup sugar**
1   **envelope unflavored gelatine**
¼   **teaspoon salt**
2   **teaspoons grated orange rind**
⅓   **cup orange juice**
3   **eggs, separated**
1   **tablespoon fresh lemon juice**
½   **cup Dry Sherry**
1   **cup whipping cream**
1   **(3 ounce) package lady fingers**
1   **(10 ounce) package frozen raspberries, thawed**

Combine sugar, gelatine, salt and orange rind in top of double boiler. Stir in orange juice and lightly beaten egg yolks. Place over hot water; cook, stirring frequently, until mixture thickens, about 10 to 15 minutes. Remove from heat; stir in lemon juice and sherry. Cool until slightly thickened. Beat egg whites until stiff; whip cream. Fold egg whites and cream into gelatine mixture. Line a 8 or 9-inch spring form pan with lady fingers with tips cut off. Carefully pour gelatine mixture into pan. Chill until firm. Cut into wedges and serve with thawed raspberries.

Noni Vera's Torte

2 cups cooked Swiss chard, chopped, or 3 frozen packages chard
1 onion, chopped
2 cloves garlic, chopped fine
1 teaspoon parsley
¼ teaspoon thyme
½ cup bread crumbs
1 cup raisins, dark or white
½ cup pine nuts
½ cup grated Parmesan cheese
½ cup sugar
1 cup half and half cream
6 eggs
1 teaspoon salt
¼ teaspoon pepper
dash of allspice or nutmeg

Crust:

3 cups flour
2 teaspoons baking powder
3 tablespoons sugar
¼ teaspoon salt
¼ cup rum
4 eggs
5 tablespoons butter, melted
¼ cup half and half cream
¼ cup chopped walnuts (optional)
1 square chocolate, grated
granulated sugar

Cook chard. Cool, drain, and squeeze dry. Sauté onion and garlic; sprinkle in parsley and thyme. Combine with bread crumbs and chard and mix well. Add raisins, pine nuts, cheese, sugar, cream, eggs, seasonings, and spices. Mix well.

Crust: Combine all ingredients and mix well until of kneading consistency. Knead a few times. Use very little flour when rolling dough to size. Oil two pie tins and line with dough. Be sure to roll out dough big enough as it has an elastic quality. Put in filling, making sure dough does not extend over edge of pan. Sprinkle walnuts and chocolate and a little sugar over each torte. Bake at 375 degrees for 20 minutes, then reduce heat to 325 degrees and bake for an additional 20 minutes. Makes 2 tortes.

More sugar may be added if you like. My family doesn't like this too sweet, but maybe yours will, so cook to please their tastes. Sometimes I add a little pork sausage meat to the torte mixture. ¼ cup meat, chopped fine and sautéed, is sufficient.

Poppy Seed Torte

⅓ cup poppy seed
¾ cup milk
¾ cup butter
1½ cups sugar
1½ teaspoons vanilla
2 cups flour
2½ teaspoons baking powder
¼ teaspoon salt
4 egg whites

Soak poppy seed in milk for 1 hour. Cream butter and gradually add sugar, creaming well. Stir in vanilla, poppy seeds, and milk. Sift together flour, baking powder, and salt; stir into creamed mixture. Fold in beaten egg whites. Pour into two well-greased and lightly-floured round cake pans. Bake at 375 degrees for 20-25 minutes. Let cool 10 minutes in pans. Remove to racks.

Filling:
½ cup sugar
1 tablespoon cornstarch
1½ cups milk
4 egg yolks, slightly beaten
1 teaspoon vanilla
¼ cup chopped walnuts
¼ cup powdered sugar

Filling: Mix sugar with cornstarch. Combine with milk and egg yolks. Cook and stir until mixture thickens and boils (about 1 minute). Cool slightly, then add vanilla and nuts. Cool thoroughly.

Split each cake into 2 layers. Assemble torte, spreading the filling between the layers. Sift powdered sugar over top. Chill 2-3 hours before serving.

Schaum Torte (MERINGUE)

6 egg whites
2 cups granulated sugar
2 teaspoons vinegar
1 teaspoon vanilla
½ pint whipping cream, sweetened
berries or fruit of your choice

Beat egg whites until stiff. Beat in sugar 2 tablespoons at a time, beating thoroughly after each addition. Add vinegar and vanilla, blending well. Pour into greased spring form pan and bake at 250 degrees for 1 hour. Turn off oven and let torte cool in oven with door open for at least 1 hour. Remove from oven; torte will have a light airy crust from baking. Remove this crust carefully and fill torte with whipped cream and berries or other fruit. Replace crust and serve.

For a variation, use ice cream in place of the whipped cream.

Sally's Ranch Cookies

2   cups shortening
2   cups white sugar
2   cups brown sugar
4   eggs
2   teaspoons vanilla
4   tablespoons water
4   cups flour
2   teaspoons soda
2   teaspoons baking powder
1   teaspoon salt
4   cups Quick Oats
4   cups Rice Krispies
1   cup chopped walnuts (optional)

Cream shortening well, add white sugar and brown sugar slowly until thoroughly blended. Add eggs, one at a time, and beat well. Add water. Sift flour, then measure and combine with soda, baking powder and salt and add to creamed mixture. Fold in oats and Rice Krispies— nuts, if desired. Bake for 10-15 minutes at 350° F. Yield about 16 dozen.

Nutty Nougats

1   cup butter
¼   cup powdered sugar
½   teaspoon salt
1   teaspoon vanilla
1   tablespoon water
2   cups sifted enriched flour
1   cup chopped pecans or walnuts

Cream butter and powdered sugar thoroughly. Add salt, vanilla, water and flour and blend well. Add nuts. Form into small balls or rolls the size of a finger. Bake on ungreased cookie sheet in 300 degree oven for about 15 minutes.

For a light dessert, slice fresh peaches into a deep glass bowl and sprinkle with sugar. Pour over Sebastiani Chenin Blanc in whatever amount you desire. Stir lightly, chill, and serve. The wine gives the peaches a special flavor and also keeps them from discoloring.

Raisin Crispies

¾ cup raisins
½ cup shortening
¼ cup water
1 teaspoon vanilla
1 cup brown sugar
¾ cup flour
½ teaspoon salt
½ teaspoon soda
½ teaspoon cinnamon
1½ cups rolled oats, uncooked—
(quick type)

Rinse and drain raisins. Combine with shortening and water and heat only until shortening melts, stirring constantly. Let cool. Stir in vanilla and sugar. Sift flour with salt, soda, and cinnamon. Stir into raisin mixture, blending well. Stir in oats. Drop by teaspoonfuls onto greased cookie sheet. Bake at 350 degrees for 10 minutes. Makes about 4 dozen small cookies.

Apple Torte

2½ cups graham cracker crumbs, about 24 crackers
¼ cup butter
½ teaspoon cinnamon
3 eggs, separated
1 can Eagle Brand condensed milk
2 tablespoons lemon juice
1 can applesauce
½ pint whipping cream

Blend 2 cups crumbs with butter and cinnamon. Use this to line a greased spring form pan. Beat egg yolks until thick; stir in milk carefully. Alternately mix lemon juice and applesauce into milk and egg yolk mixture. Beat egg whites stiff and fold gently into mixture. Pour into pan and sprinkle with remaining crumbs. Bake at 350 degrees for 50 minutes. Top with whipped cream before serving.

Helen's Maple Nut Torte

4 eggs, separated
1½ cups maple syrup
½ teaspoon salt
2 envelopes unflavored gelatine
½ cup water
2 cups whipped cream
20 macaroons, dried in a low oven and rolled into crumbs
10-15 whole macaroons
1½ cups chopped nuts

Beat egg yolks slightly; add maple syrup and salt and cook on top of a double boiler until of custard consistency, stirring frequently. Soften gelatine in water, add to hot maple custard and stir until dissolved. Cool custard, then add whipped cream, macaroon crumbs, and nuts. Fold in stiffly-beaten egg whites. Pour into a 10" spring form pan that has been lined with whole macaroons. Chill overnight and before unmolding for serving, top with more whipped cream and nuts if desired.

Steamed Carrot Pudding

1   cup grated raw carrots
1   cup grated potatoes
1   cup sugar
½   cup butter
2   eggs
1   cup flour
1   teaspoon baking soda
1   teaspoon cloves
1   teaspoon cinnamon
½   teaspoon nutmeg
     salt to taste
½   cup raisins
½   cup currants
½   cup walnuts

Mix carrots, potatoes, sugar and butter. Add eggs, flour, and soda, blending well. Add spices and after well-blended, add raisins, currants and walnuts. Put into steamer, filled about 2/3 full with water. Cover and steam in water for 2 hours. Serve with Hard Sauce (see recipe in this book).

Steamed Cranberry Pudding

2   tablespoons butter
¾   cup sugar
1   egg, beaten
2   cups flour
4   teaspoon baking powder
½   teaspoon salt
1   cup milk
3½   tablespoons orange juice
½   teaspoon grated orange rind
1   cup raw cranberries, cut in pieces

Butter Sauce:

½   cup sugar
½   cup cream
½   cup butter

Cream butter and sugar; add egg. Sift flour, baking powder, and salt. Add this alternately with milk to creamed mixture. Add orange juice and rind. Mix well. Then add cranberries. Put into steamer about 2/3 full with water and steam for 2 hours.

Prepare sauce by mixing sugar, cream, and butter. Stir together and cook over boiling water for 15 minutes. Use as topping for pudding.

Rice Pudding

6   eggs
1   quart milk
     pinch of salt
1   cup sugar
1   teaspoon vanilla
2   cups rice, cooked
½   cup currants

Put eggs, milk, salt, and sugar together and beat well. Add vanilla, rice, and currants and mix well. Place in a baking dish. Place this dish in a shallow pan with water and bake in a 300 degree oven for 1 hour. Serves 8-10.

Persimmon Pudding

2　cups persimmon pulp
3　eggs
1¼　cups sugar
1½　cups flour
1　teaspoon baking powder
1　teaspoon baking soda
½　teaspoon salt
½　cup melted butter
1　teaspoon vanilla
2½　cups milk
2　teaspoons cinnamon
1　teaspoon ginger (optional)
½　teaspoon nutmeg
½　cup raisins
½　cup chopped walnuts

Hard sauce (see recipe in this book)

Combine all ingredients together and mix well. Bake in a greased 9X9 baking dish for 1 hour at 325 degrees until firm. Top with Hard sauce before serving.

Zabaglione Classic

6　egg yolks
½　cup sugar
¼　cup Sebastiani Johannisberg Riesling or August Sebastiani Country Chenin Blanc
　grated rind and juice of 1 lemon
　touch of brandy (optional)

Measure ingredients into top of double boiler and place over boiling water. Beat constantly with a rotary beater until mixture thickens and mounds like whipped cream. Remove from heat. Serve hot or chilled in tall parfait glasses alone or as a topping for sponge cake or canned fruit. Makes about 4 servings.

This very old Italian dessert is excellent after a heavy dinner. It is especially nice because it can be made on the spur of the moment.

Cakes

Suggestions

1. When baking cakes, place layer pans in the center of oven or space them so that even baking is assured.

2. Don't adhere strictly to suggested baking times given in recipes. Always test cakes for doneness. When a toothpick comes out clean, the cake is done. Or you can touch the cake lightly on top: if it springs back, it is done; if the impression of your finger remains, bake a few minutes longer.

3. Do not overbake cake or it will be crusty and have a poor texture.

4. If cake has a tendency to stick to the pan, wrap a towel dipped in hot water around the pan after it is removed from the oven. You will be able to remove the cake to a rack in just a few minutes.

5. While cake mixes are popular because they are time-saving and economical, they can never equal a cake produced from scratch using fresh ingredients. If you do use a packaged cake mix, add ¼ cup of any cooking oil to the batter. This will insure that the cake will stay fresh and moist.

6. When using packaged cake mixes, you can improve the cake tremendously if you split the layers and spread with pudding mixes. I usually fill a chocolate cake with chocolate pudding and a white cake with vanilla or lemon pudding. Simply cook pudding according to directions given on pudding package, but decrease amount of milk from 2 cups to 1¾ cups. It takes two packages of pudding mix to fill a cake with four layers (2 regular layers split into halves). After assembling cake, frost with your favorite frosting and serve.

7. Packaged cake mixes can be quite versatile if you use a little creativity. For a banana nutmeg cake, simply mix 1 package of yellow cake mix as directed on package, adding ⅛ teaspoon baking soda and ½ teaspoon nutmeg and substitute 1 cup mashed bananas for half of the water called for in the recipe. After baking, fill and frost with the frosting of your choice.

Another variation is to substitute 2/3 cup drained, crushed pineapple for 1/3 of the water needed in a yellow cake mix. Also add 2 teaspoons grated lemon rind to mix before pouring into cake pans. Frost as you wish.

As a general rule, substitute ½ cup of whatever juice or liquid you desire for ½ cup of water called for in the directions given on the package of cake mix. This will give your cakes a different flavor without having to bake from scratch.

Angel Cake Cloud

1	10 in. angel food cake
1	pt. whipping cream
1	package frozen strawberries
1	cup small marshmallows
1	small can crushed pineapple, well-drained

Beat cream until firm. Fold in fruits and marshmallows. Split cake into 3 layers and put cream mixed with fruit between layers and on top.

Wine Angel Cake

1	10 inch angel food cake
10	tablespoons Sebastiani Chenin Blanc or August Sebastiani Country Chenin Blanc
2	cups sour cream
1	cup sifted powdered sugar
1	3 oz. package cream cheese

Split cake in half horizontally. Sprinkle bottom half with 5 tablespoons of wine, then spread 1 cup of sour cream over it and dust with ½ cup sugar. Replace top of cake. Pour remaining wine over entire cake. Blend cream cheese with remaining sour cream and sugar. Use this as frosting spreading over cake. Chill 4 hours.

Bourbon Ice-box Cake

3	packages unflavored gelatine
½	cup cold water
	boiling water
6	eggs, separated
4	tablespoons bourbon
1	cup sugar
1	tablespoon lemon juice
1	pt. whipping cream
2	packages lady fingers

Soak gelatine in cold water for 5 minutes, then fill with boiling water until there is 1 cup. Stir to dissolve gelatine. Cool until mixture begins to congeal. Beat egg yolks until thick and lemon-colored, adding bourbon slowly while beating. Beat in sugar and continue beating until mixture is very light. Add lemon juice. Whip cream and fold in. Beat egg whites stiff and fold in. Line bottom and sides of a spring form mold with lady fingers. Pour filling into mold and let chill several hours or overnight.

Brandy Cake

1½ cups seedless raisins
1½ cups water
¾ cup butter
1½ cups sugar
2 eggs
2¼ cups flour
1½ teaspoons baking soda
1 teaspoon baking powder
¾ cup brandy
¾ cup ground nuts
   nutmeg and cinnamon to taste

Frosting:
1 cube butter
1 egg yolk, beaten
1½ cups powdered sugar
4 tablespoons brandy

Boil raisins and water together until it yields ¾ cup. Drain and keep water. Cool raisins and chop. Cream butter and add sugar. Beat eggs into this. Sift together flour, soda, and baking powder. Add to the first mixture along with water from the raisins and brandy. Add raisins, nuts, nutmeg, and cinnamon. Bake at 350 degrees for 35 minutes in 2 layer pans.

Frosting: Cream butter along with egg yolk and sugar. Use brandy to moisten. Spread on cooled cake layers.

Cheese Cake

1¾ cups graham cracker crumbs
¼-½ cup nuts
½ teaspoon cinnamon
½ cup butter, melted
3 eggs, well-beaten
2 8 oz. packages cream cheese
1 cup sugar
¼ teaspoon salt
2 teaspoons vanilla
½ teaspoon almond extract
3 cups sour cream

Combine cracker crumbs, nuts, and cinnamon with melted butter. Line sides and bottom of spring form pan with this mixture. In mixing bowl, combine eggs, cheese, sugar, salt, vanilla, and almond extract. Beat until smooth. Blend in sour cream. Pour into pan and bake at 375 degrees for 35 minutes. Cool 4-5 hours.

Crazy Cake

1 package yellow cake mix
¾ cup oil
¾ cup water
1 package lemon jello
4 eggs

Frosting:
1 cup powdered sugar
   juice of 1 lemon

In a mixing bowl, blend cake mix, oil, water, and jello. Add eggs one at a time and beat for 4 minutes. Bake in a greased and floured 9 x 9 inch pan for 40-45 minutes at 350 degrees.

Frosting: Mix powdered sugar and lemon juice thoroughly and spread on hot cake. Serve hot.

Carrot Cake

1¾ cups sugar
1¼ cups vegetable oil
4 eggs
2 cups flour
2 teaspoons soda
2 teaspoons baking powder
1 teaspoon salt
3 cups grated carrots
½ cup shredded coconut
1 cup walnuts

Frosting
1 8 oz. package cream cheese
2 teaspoons vanilla
¼ cup butter
1 lb. package powdered sugar
½ cup crushed pineapple, drained

Grease and flour 3 eight inch layer pans. Cream sugar and oil. Add eggs one at a time and beat thoroughly. Sift together flour, soda, baking powder, and salt. Add to egg mixture. Fold in carrots, coconut, and nuts. Pour into pans and bake at 325 degrees for 30 minutes.

Frosting: In electric mixer, blend all ingredients together and spread on cooled cake layers.

Coffee Cake

2½ cups flour
¾ cup sugar
¼ teaspoon nutmeg
 pinch of salt
1 cup brown sugar
¾ cup oil
1 egg
1 cup buttermilk or sour milk
1 teaspoon baking soda
1 teaspoon baking powder
1 cup chopped nuts (optional)
 cinnamon (optional)

Mix flour, sugar, nutmeg, salt, brown sugar, and oil thoroughly. Save ½ cup of this mixture for the topping. Mix egg, milk, soda and baking powder together and add to the flour mixture, stirring well. Pour into a greased and floured 9 x 9 inch pan, then sprinkle with topping. Add chopped nuts and sprinkle with cinnamon, if desired. Bake at 325 degrees for 45 minutes. Serves 8-10.

Easy Devil Food Cake

5   rounded tablespoons cocoa
⅔   cup water
     pinch of salt
½   cup shortening
2   cups sugar
3   eggs
1   cup sour milk
2   level teaspoons soda
3   tablespoons hot water
2   cups flour
1   teaspoon vanilla

Frosting:
½   pt. whipping cream
1   tablespoon powdered sugar
1   tablespoon cocoa

Cook cocoa, water, and salt together for 3 minutes. Let cool. Cream shortening and sugar. Add eggs and cocoa mixture. Then add sour milk and mix well. Dissolve soda in hot water and add to mixture. Then add flour and vanilla, mixing well. Bake in greased and floured loaf pan at 350 degrees for 40 minutes.

Frosting: Beat cream until thick. Add sugar and cocoa and mix until well--blended. Spread over cake.

Date Cake

1   cup pitted dates,
     cut into sixths
1   cup water
½   teaspoon baking soda
½   cup butter
1   cup sugar
2   eggs
1½   cups flour
1½   teaspoons baking powder
1   teaspoon cinnamon
1   teaspoon salt
1   teaspoon vanilla
1½   cups nut meats, chopped (optional)

Frosting:
1   cup water
½   cup brown sugar
½   cup white sugar
½   cup walnut meats, chopped

Place dates in a bowl. Bring water to a boil in saucepan. Add soda, stir until dissolved. Pour water over dates and let cool. Cream together butter and sugar. Add eggs one at a time, beating well. Sift flour with baking powder, cinnamon, and salt. Add to creamed mixture alternately with the water poured off from the dates. Beat well after each addition. Stir in dates, vanilla, and nuts. Spread in a well-greased 9 inch square pan. Bake at 350 degrees for 40 minutes.

Frosting: Boil all ingredients together for 10 mins. Continue cooking until mixture is thick. Pour over cooled cake.

Egyptian Cake

5   tablespoons chocolate
5   tablespoons boiling water
½   cup butter
1½   cups sugar
4   eggs, separated
½   cup milk
1¾   cups flour
2   teaspoons baking powder
     pinch of salt
1   teaspoon vanilla

Filling:
2   eggs, separated
     pinch of salt
1   cup finely chopped nuts
5   tablespoons powdered sugar
1   cup whipping cream
1   teaspoon vanilla

Dissolve chocolate in boiling water. Cream butter, adding sugar gradually. Add beaten egg yolks, milk and blend well. Add chocolate. Mix and sift flour with baking powder and pinch of salt. Add to creamed mixture. Beat egg whites until stiff and flavor with vanilla. Fold gently into cake batter. Pour into greased and well-floured cake pans and bake at 350 degrees for 25-30 minutes.

Filling: Beat egg yolks until creamy and thick. Add salt, nuts, and sugar. Beat egg whites until stiff and fold into egg yolks. Whip cream and pour egg white mixture into it. Flavor with vanilla. If not thick enough, add more powdered sugar. Spread between layers of cooled cake.

Elegant Cheese Cake

1½   cups Zwieback crumbs
¼   cup melted butter
4   tablespoons sugar
4   tablespoons finely ground
     unblanched almonds
2   tablespoons heavy cream
5   eggs
1   cup sugar
1½   lb. cottage cheese, put
     through a sieve
¼   cup flour
½   pint heavy cream
½   teaspoon salt
     juice and rind of 1 lemon
1   can cherry pie filling (optional)

Combine crumbs, butter, sugar, almonds, and 2 tablespoons cream. Press mixture thickly against the bottom and sides of a well-buttered 9-inch spring form pan. Beat eggs until thick and lemon colored. Add sugar gradually, then add cheese, and beat well. Add flour, cream, salt, and lemon. Pour carefully into pan and bake at 325 degrees for 45 minutes, until firm. Turn off heat, open oven door, and let cake cool in the oven. Spread cherry filling over chilled cake before serving, if desired.

Fruit Cocktail Cake

1 cup flour
1 cup sugar
1 teaspoon soda
½ teaspoon salt
1 egg, beaten
1 large can fruit cocktail, well-drained
½ cup brown sugar
½ cup chopped nuts
½ pint whipping cream

Combine flour, sugar, soda and salt. Add egg and fruit cocktail. Pour mixture into well-greased, shallow 9 inch square pan. Mix together brown sugar and nuts and pour over cake mixture. Bake at 300 degrees for 1 hour. Serve topped with whipped cream. Serves 6-8.

Graham Cracker Cake

½ cup butter
1 cup sugar
3 eggs, separated
⅔ cup milk
½ teaspoon salt
25 honey-flavored graham crackers
2½ teaspoons baking powder
1 cup chopped nuts
1 teaspoon vanilla
1 pt. whipping cream

Cream butter and sugar. Add beaten egg yolks, milk, and salt and beat well. Finely crush graham crackers, mix with baking powder, and add to cream mixture. Add ½ cup nuts and vanilla. Fold in stiffly-beaten egg whites. Pour into 2 layer pans, greased and well-floured. bake at 350 degrees for 20-25 minutes. Let cool. Fill and top with unsweetened whipped cream and sprinkle with remaining nuts.

Lady Baltimore Cake

3	cups flour
3	teaspoons baking powder
¼	teaspoon salt
½	cup butter
1½	cups sugar
½	cup milk
½	cup water
1	teaspoon vanilla
¼	teaspoon almond extract
3	egg whites, stiffly-beaten

Frosting:

½	cup sugar
⅔	cup boiling water
1	teaspoon vanilla
½	teaspoon corn syrup
2	egg whites, stiffly beaten
½	cup raisins, chopped
6	figs, chopped
½	cup walnut or pecan meats, chopped

Sift flour, baking powder and salt together. Cream butter thoroughly and add sugar gradually, creaming until light and fluffy. Add flour mixture alternately with milk and water, a small amount at a time. Beat well after each addition. Continue in this manner until all flour and liquid has been blended. Add vanilla and almond extract; then fold in egg whites quickly and thoroughly. Bake in 2 greased 9 inch layer pans at 350 degrees for 20 minutes.

Frosting: Combine sugar, water and corn syrup. Bring quickly to a boil until a small amount of syrup forms a soft ball in cold water. Pour syrup in a fine stream over egg whites and beat constantly. Add vanilla and beat with a rotary beater 10-15 minutes until frosting is of spreading consistency. Add raisins, figs, and nuts and blend well. Fill and frost cooled layers of cake.

Lemon Chiffon Ice Box Cake

8	eggs, separated
1½	cups sugar
	juice from 2 lemons
1	envelope unflavored gelatine
1	cup cold water
½	cup boiling water
1	6 oz. package lady fingers (3 doz.)
½	pt. whipping cream

Beat egg yolks until light in color. Add ½ cup sugar and lemon juice. Cook in top of double boiler until thick. Soak gelatine in cold water about 10 minutes. Dissolve in boiling water and add to custard slowly. Beat egg whites until stiff and fold in the remaining sugar. Then fold into custard. Line a spring form pan with lady fingers and pour custard in. Chill overnight and top with whipped cream before serving.

Mayonnaise Cake

1	teaspoon soda
1	cup boiling water
1	cup walnuts, chopped
½	cup dates, cut up
½	cup raisins
1	cup sugar
1	teaspoon cinnamon
3	tablespoons cocoa
1	cup mayonnaise
1¾	cups flour
1	teaspoon salt
1	teaspoon vanilla
	powdered sugar

Dissolve soda in water. Pour over nuts, dates, and raisins. Let stand. Sift sugar, cinnamon, and cocoa together. Stir in mayonnaise and drained nuts, dates, and raisins. Blend well. Sift flour and salt together and add to mayonnaise mixture. Add vanilla and mix well. Pour into greased and floured 8 x 13 inch pan and bake at 350 degrees 30-40 minutes. Cover with powdered sugar before serving.

Meringue Cake

½	cup butter
1½	cups sugar
4	eggs, separated
2	teaspoons vanilla
5	tablespoons milk
1	cup flour
1	teaspoon baking powder
¼	teaspoon salt
¼	teaspoon cream of tartar

Filling:
4	tablespoons sugar
2	tablespoons cornstarch
½	teaspoon salt
2	egg yolks
2	cups milk
½	teaspoon vanilla
½	pt. whipping cream
1	cup strawberries

Cream butter and ½ cup sugar. Add 4 egg yolks, well-beaten, and 1 teaspoon vanilla. Add milk alternately to creamed mixture with flour, baking powder, and salt sifted together. Spread batter in thin layers in 2 layer pans, greased, well-floured, and lined with wax paper, also greased and well-floured. Beat egg whites until they peak, then add cream of tartar. Beat in 1 cup sugar slowly and thoroughly. Add 1 teaspoon vanilla, blend well, and spread mixture on top of cake batter. Bake at 325 degrees for 30 minutes.

Filling: Combine sugar, cornstarch and salt together. Stir in egg yolks and add milk. Cook over low heat, stirring until thick, and then add vanilla. Remove cakes from pans. Spread filling over 1 layer and place other layer carefully on top. Whip cream and spread over top. Garnish with strawberries.

Pineapple Upside-down Cake

¼   cup butter
2   cups brown sugar
1   large can pineapple slices, drained
½   cup maraschino cherries, drained
½   cup chopped walnuts
1   package yellow cake mix
½   pt. whipping cream

Melt butter in a deep, heavy iron skillet and spread all around the sides of the skillet. Cover with brown sugar, spreading evenly. Place 1 pineapple slice in the center and cut rest of the slices in half, crosswise. Arrange these in a circle around the center slice like the spokes of a wheel, rounded edges facing one way. Fill spaces with cherries and nuts. Prepare cake batter as indicated on package. Pour over pineapples, cherries, and nuts. Bake at 350 degrees for 30-40 minutes until firm. Cool only for a couple of minutes. Place serving dish over skillet and turn upside down to remove cake. Let cool and serve with whipped cream.

Potato Cake

2   cups sugar
⅔   cup butter
4   eggs (beaten)
1   cup mashed potatoes
½   cup ground chocolate (dry)
½   cup milk
2   cups flour
3½   teaspoons baking powder
¼   teaspoon salt
½   teaspoon cloves
1   teaspoon cinnamon
1   teaspoon nutmeg
1   cup chopped walnuts

Frosting:
2   cubes butter, softened
1   cup powdered sugar
4   tablespoons ground chocolate (dry)
4   tablespoons boiling water
    chopped walnuts (optional)

Grease and flour 2 layer pans. Cream sugar and butter. Mix together eggs, potatoes, chocolate, milk, flour, baking powder, salt, and spices. Add to creamed mixture, then add nuts lastly. Pour into pans and bake at 350 degrees for 30 minutes.

Frosting: Cream butter with sugar and chocolate. Add water and beat well with rotary beater until smooth. Spread between cooled cake layers and on top. Garnish with nuts if desired.

Powdered Sugar Pound Cake

3   cubes butter
1   box powdered sugar
6   eggs
1   teaspoon vanilla
2¾   cups flour

Beat butter in a large bowl. Add sugar and beat until creamy and fluffy. Add eggs one at a time, beating well after each egg. Add vanilla. Sift and measure flour and add gradually to mixture. Bake at 300 degrees in a greased tube pan for 1½ hours. Check cake in 1 hour. (This can also be baked in 2 loaf pans; if so, less baking time is required.)

Prune Cake

½   cup butter
1   cup sugar
2   eggs
1½   cups flour
1   teaspoon cinnamon
1   teaspoon cloves
½   teaspoon salt
1   teaspoon soda
2   teaspoons baking powder
1½   tablespoons cornstarch
¾   cup sour cream
1   cup stewed prunes, chopped
2   tablespoons prune juice
½   cup chopped walnuts

Filling:
2   eggs beaten
1   cup sugar
½   cup sour cream
½   teaspoon salt
1   cup stewed prunes, chopped
2   tablespoons butter
½   pt. whipping cream

Cream butter and sugar. Add eggs and beat well. Add dry ingredients and sour cream, blending well. Then add prunes and prune juice. Add nuts last. Pour into 2 greased and well-floured cake pans and bake at 325 degrees for 30-35 minutes.

Filling: Mix all ingredients together in upper part of a double boiler and cook until very thick, stirring frequently. Let cool, then spread between the cooled cake layers. Top with whipped cream before serving.

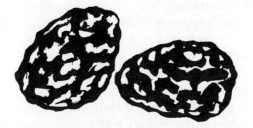

Rum Cake

½   cup shortening
2   cups sugar
1   teaspoon vanilla
1   jigger rum
4   eggs
3   cups flour
½   teaspoon salt
½   teaspoon baking powder
½   teaspoon baking soda
1   cup buttermilk

Topping:
1   cube butter
1   cup sugar
1   teaspoon vanilla
1   jigger rum

Cream shortening, sugar, vanilla, and rum together with electric mixer. Add eggs one at a time, beating well. Sift flour, salt, and baking powder together. Add soda to buttermilk. Add small amount of flour mixture to creamed mixture, followed by a small amount of milk, mixing well. Continue in this manner until all flour and milk have been added. Grease a tube pan and pour batter into it. Bake at 325 degrees for 1 hour.

Topping: Melt all ingredients together. Remove cake from oven, leave in pan, and place on large plate. Pour topping over cake and let stand 4 hours before serving.

Ice Box Cake

2   dozen lady fingers
4   packages vanilla Whip n' Chill
2   cups milk
1   cup Sebastiani Chenin Blanc
     or August Sebastiani Country
     Chenin Blanc
1   cup whipping cream
1   can mandarin oranges (optional)

Line a spring form pan, sides and bottom, with lady fingers. Beat Whip n' Chill with milk, then slowly beat in wine. Beat cream until stiff and fold into Whip n' Chill mixture. Spoon into spring form pan. If desired decorate with oranges. Chill. Serves 12-14.

This dessert can easily be made a few days prior to serving and frozen.

Wine Cake

1   package yellow cake mix
¾   cup oil
¾   cup Sebastiani Chenin Blanc
     or August Sebastiani Country
     Chenin Blanc
4   eggs
1   package vanilla pudding
¾   teaspoon nutmeg
Frosting:
1   cube butter
1   package powdered sugar
¼   cup Arenas Dry Sherry or Amore
     Cream Sherry

In mixing bowl, place cake mix, oil, and sherry. Blend well, then add eggs one at a time, mixing well after each addition. Then add vanilla pudding and nutmeg and beat 4 minutes at medium speed. Bake for 45 minutes at 350 degrees in a tube pan, greased and floured.

Frosting: Cream butter and add sugar gradually. Add sherry and blend well. Spread over cooled cake and serve.

Pies

Suggestions

1. You will have one less bowl to wash if you mix the pie dough in the pie pan. Just remember to wipe the pan out with a paper towel after removing dough to the rolling board.

2. The dough for pie crust is always much easier to handle if it is chilled for 30 minutes prior to rolling.

3. Brush bottom crust of fruit and berry pies with soft butter and let harden before filling. This prevents the crust from getting soggy.

4. Make apple pies with apple cubes instead of slices. The cubes support the top crust better and they also allow sugar and seasonings to spread through the pie.

5. Baking time for a pumpkin pie can be halved if the filling is readied and set into a pan of boiling water, stirring occasionally. Place pie crust into heated oven for 10 minutes, then pour warm filling into the partially baked crust. Return pie to oven and reduce baking time to half the time indicated in the recipe.

6. If juices from fruit pies bubble over during baking, sprinkle spilled juice with salt to prevent smoke and odor.

7. When pressed for time, instead of making a regulation pie, just make up the filling, pour into custard cups and top with a meringue. Place the cups into the oven and brown the meringue, then cool. This trick can be used only with such fillings as are poured into cooked pastry shells, e.g., lemon, chocolate, butterscotch, and the like.

Pie Crust

2   cups flour
1   teaspoon baking powder
     dash of salt
⅔   cup of Crisco
5-6 tablespoons ice water

Sift flour, baking powder, and salt into a bowl. Add Crisco, cutting into pieces in flour mixture. Add 1 tablespoon water at a time and blend well. Roll quite thick. Makes 2 crusts.

Angel Pie

Shell:
4   egg whites
½   teaspoon cream of tartar
1   cup sugar

Filling:
4   egg yolks
½   cup sugar
3   tablespoons lemon juice
2   teaspoons grated lemon rind
1   cup whipping cream

Beat egg whites until foamy, then beat in cream of tartar. Gradually add sugar and beat stiff. Spread in a slightly buttered 9 inch pie plate. Bake at 300 degrees for 40 minutes. Let cool while making the filling.

Filling: Beat egg yolks until thick and lemon colored. Beat in sugar, lemon juice, and rind. Cook in a double boiler until thick. Cool. Fold in stiffly-whipped cream. Pour into cooled pie shell and chill for 24 hours.

Apple Pie

    pastry for 2 crust pie (see Pie
    Crust recipe in this book)
6   medium-sized apples
½-⅔ cup sugar
⅛   teaspoon salt
1   tablespoon flour
¼   teaspoon cinnamon
⅛   teaspoon nutmeg
1   tablespoon lemon juice
1-2 tablespoons butter
    melted butter

Line pie pan with half the pastry. Peel, core, and cut apples into cubes. Place cubes into a large bowl and add sugar, salt, flour, spices and lemon juice. Mix ingredients very gently until apple cubes are well-coated. Then pour into pie pan and dot with butter. Cover with top crust and brush melted butter over crust. Bake 10 minutes at 425 degrees, then reduce heat to 350 degrees and bake for an additional 45 minutes to 1 hour.

Applesauce Cream Pie

1   baked pie shell
2   tablespoons unflavored gelatine
4   tablespoons water
2   egg yolks, well-beaten
¼   cup sugar
1   tablespoon flour
1¼   cup scalded milk
½   teaspoon vanilla
¼   teaspoon salt
2½   cups thick, sweetened apple sauce
2   tablespoons lemon juice
½   pt. whipping cream (optional)

Soften gelatine in cold water. Combine egg yolks, sugar, and flour and beat thoroughly. Add milk slowly, stirring constantly. Cook over hot water until thick, stirring frequently. Remove from heat, add gelatine and let cool. Mix together vanilla, salt, applesauce, and lemon juice. Add to cooled milk mixture carefully. Pour into pie shell and chill. Serve with or without whipped cream.

Black Bottom Pie

Crust:
17   graham crackers
¼   cup sugar
½   cup butter, melted

Crush crackers very fine. Add sugar and butter and mix well. Pat firmly into pie pan to form crust. Bake 12-15 minutes at 400 degrees until brown.

Filling:
1   envelope unflavored gelatine
¼   cup cold water
4   eggs, separated
2   cups scalded milk
1   cup sugar
1½   tablespoons cornstarch
1½   squares baking chocolate, melted
2   teaspoons vanilla
¼   teaspoon cream of tartar
½   pt. whipping cream
1   square baking chocolate, grated

Filling: Mix gelatine in cold water and set aside. Beat egg yolks and slowly add to scalded milk in top of double boiler. Add ½ cup sugar; then add cornstarch mixed with a little cold water and let simmer 20 minutes. Add gelatine mixture and mix well. Remove from fire and take out 1 cup of custard mixture. To this, add chocolate and 1 teaspoon vanilla. Place in pie crust and chill. Beat egg whites, add cream of tartar, then gradually add ½ cup sugar and 1 teaspoon vanilla, beating slowly. Fold egg white mixture into custard and spread over the chocolate layer of pie. Top with whipped cream and sprinkle with chocolate.

Coffee Sponge Pie

1   baked 9-inch pie shell
1   tablespoon unflavored gelatine
¼   cup cold water
3   eggs, separated
1   cup sugar
1   cup very strong coffee
¼   teaspoon salt
1   teaspoon vanilla
½   pt. whipping cream

Soften gelatine in water and set aside. Beat egg yolks until light and lemon-colored; gradually beat in ½ cup sugar. Add coffee slowly, then salt. Place over boiling water and cook 5 minutes, or until thick, stirring constantly. Add softened gelatine and stir until gelatine is dissolved. Chill until mixture begins to thicken. Gradually beat remaining sugar into stiffly-beaten egg whites. Add vanilla, then fold into slightly-thickened coffee-gelatine mixture. Turn into pie shell and chill until firm. Cover with whipped cream when ready to serve.

Creme de Menthe Pie

30 marshmallows
1   cup milk
2-4 tablespoons creme
    de menthe, green
½   pt. whipping cream
1   cube butter
1   package chocolate wafers, crushed

Melt marshmallows in 1 cup milk over double boiler. Let cool. Add creme de menthe. Whip cream and fold into marshmallows. Melt butter and make pie crust by adding crushed wafers and molding into pie tin. Fill with marshmallow mixture and chill.

Cherry Chiffon Pie

1   baked pie shell
1   envelope plain unflavored gelatine
¼   cup cold water
1   cup sugar
½   cup cherry juice from 1
    can of sour pitted cherries
½   teaspoon salt
4   eggs, separated
½   teaspoon grated lemon rind
½   pt. whipping cream

Combine gelatine and cold water and let stand until thick. Combine ½ cup sugar, cherry juice, salt, and beaten egg yolks in the top of a double boiler. Cook over boiling water until thick and of a custard consistency. Add gelatine and lemon rind; cool until lukewarm. Beat egg whites with ½ cup sugar until stiff. Fold into custard mixture. Fill pie shell and set in a cool place until firm. Top with whipped cream and cherries.

Eggnog Pie

1   baked pie shell
1   teaspoon unflavored gelatine
1   tablespoon cold water
1   cup milk
½   cup sugar
2   tablespoons cornstarch
¼   teaspoon salt
3   egg yolks, beaten
1   tablespoon butter
1   teaspoon vanilla
1   cup whipped cream
     nutmeg

Soak gelatine in cold water. Combine milk, sugar, cornstarch, and salt and mix thoroughly. Put in top of double boiler and cook until thick and smooth. Cook 15 minutes longer, stirring constantly. Stir a small amount of this mixture into egg yolks, return to double boiler and cook a few minutes longer. Add gelatine and butter and let cool. Add vanilla. Fold whipped cream into custard and pour into pie shell. Sprinkle top generously with nutmeg. Chill pie until ready to serve.

Lemon Meringue Pie

1   9 in. pie shell, cooled
3   tablespoons cornstarch
1   cup plus 2 tablespoons sugar
     grated rind of 1 lemon
4   tablespoons lemon juice
1   tablespoon butter
3   eggs, separated
1½   cups boiling water
6   tablespoons sugar

Combine cornstarch with sugar in top of double boiler. Add lemon rind, lemon juice, butter, and beaten egg yolks. Mix well, then add boiling water very slowly. Cook over hot water until thick. Cool. Pour into baked pie shell. Beat egg whites until almost stiff, then add 6 tablespoons sugar while continuing to beat until stiff. Arrange on pie to entirely cover filling and bake in a 300 degree oven for 30 minutes.

Pumpkin Pie

1	large unbaked pie shell
1	can pumpkin (2 cups)
1	teaspoon salt
1½	teaspoon cinnamon
½	teaspoon cloves
½	teaspoon allspice
1	teaspoon vanilla
3	eggs
2	cups half and half cream (or milk)
1	cup brown sugar
½	pt. whipping cream
½	cup slivered almonds (optional)

Place pumpkin in electric mixer bowl along with salt, spices and vanilla. Add eggs one at a time, blending well. Add milk and sugar and mix thoroughly. Pour mixture into pie shell and bake at 425 degrees for 10 minutes. Reduce heat to 350 degrees and bake 20-30 minutes longer until pie is firm. Do not overbake. Top with whipped cream and almonds.

Ever try making a fresh pumpkin pie? You can obtain your fresh pumpkin meat in this manner: Cut pumpkin in half and remove seeds and fibers. Place on a pan in a 350 degree oven, open sides down. When both halves have collapsed, remove from oven and lift off rind. Now you can start to make your crust.

Rhubarb Pie

	pastry for 2-crust pie
3	cups rhubarb
4	tablespoons flour
1½	cups sugar
2	egg yolks, well-beaten
1	tablespoon butter

Cut rhubarb into ½ in. pieces. Sprinkle with flour, then add sugar and egg yolks and mix well. Pour into lined pie plate and dot mixture with butter. Cover with top crust or pastry strips and bake at 425 degrees for 30 minutes. Reduce heat to 325 degrees and bake another 30 minutes.

You can make a strawberry rhubarb pie by using 1½ cups strawberries and 1½ cups rhubarb for the filling.

Sherry Cream Pie

Shell:
1½   cups crushed chocolate wafer
     cookies
¼   lb. butter, melted (1 cube)

Filling:
1   envelope unflavored gelatine
1¼   cups cold milk
3   eggs, separated
½   cup sugar
⅛   teaspoon salt
¼   teaspoon nutmeg
½   cup Sherry
½   pt. whipping cream
1   square grated sweet bakers
     chocolate

Crush cookies very fine. Mix with butter and pat firmly into a 10 inch glass pie plate to form a shell. Chill 1 hour.

Filling: Soften gelatine in ¼ cup milk. Put egg yolks in top of double boiler, beating slightly. Add sugar and remaining milk; stir well and cook for 10 minutes, or until mixture coats a spoon. Remove from stove. Add gelatine, salt, and nutmeg to custard and stir until gelatine is dissolved. Add sherry slowly (so it won't curdle), stirring constantly. Place in refrigerator to thicken. Beat egg whites stiff and whip cream. Fold beaten egg whites into whipped cream gently. Fill pie shell with chilled custard mixture and top with whipped cream-egg white mixture. Sprinkle top with chocolate. Chill for 8 hours.

Strawberry Pie

1   baked pie shell
1   cup crushed strawberries, fresh
1   cup sugar
¼   teaspoon salt
1   tablespoon cornstarch
¾   cup whole fresh strawberries
½   pt. whipping cream

Mix crushed berries with sugar, salt and cornstarch. Boil until transparent. Fill pie shell with fresh whole berries, washed and hulled. Pour cooked berries over whole berries and chill. Top with whipped cream before serving.

Miscellaneous

Baked Mushrooms

1	lb. button mushrooms (sliced)
½	teaspoon powdered oregano
¼	cup cracker meal
1	tablespoon lemon juice
4	tablespoons grated Parmesan cheese
1	clove garlic, minced
2	tablespoons olive oil
	salt, pepper to taste
2	teaspoons chopped parsley

Wash and drain mushrooms. Place in shallow baking dish. Combine oregano, cracker meal, lemon juice, cheese, garlic and oil. Mix well, adding salt and pepper to taste. Sprinkle mixture over mushrooms. Bake 15 minutes at 350 degrees. Sprinkle with parsley before serving. Serves 4-6.

Bread Stuffing

1	cup chopped onion
½	cup chopped celery
2	cloves garlic (chopped)
¼	cup butter
6	cups dry bread cubes (½ in.)
¾	teaspoon salt
	dash pepper
1½	teaspoons poultry seasoning
1⅔	cup water or bouillon
½	cup chopped parsley
½	cup grated Parmesan cheese

Sauté onion, celery, and garlic in butter and combine with remaining ingredients. More water or bouillon may be added if necessary. Stuff into bird or bake in a separate baking dish for 45 minutes at 325 degrees. Makes about 4 cups.

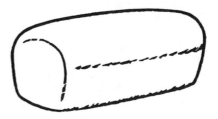

For duck or goose add ½ cup raisins to stuffing mixture.

Spanish Rolls

1	lb. Tillamook cheese
1	pimiento
1	clove garlic
2	small cans green chili peppers
1	can sliced mushrooms (optional)
2	tablespoons olive oil
2	tablespoons vinegar
1	can tomato soup, undiluted
2	dozen hot dog rolls

Put cheese, pimiento, garlic, peppers, and mushrooms through food chopper. Add oil, vinegar, and soup. Chill entire mixture. Scoop out hot dog rolls and fill with chilled mixture. Wrap in heavy wax paper, twisting at each end. Bake in covered roasting pan at 300 degrees for 45 minutes. Makes 2 dozen.

Canned Olives

1   gallon cured olives
1   gallon water
¼   lb. salt
     alum

Bring water and salt to boil in a large pot. Drop in olives and bring to second boil. After boiling, put in hot sterile quart jars. Add a pinch of alum to each jar (this keeps olives crisp) and seal.

For spiced olives, use same procedure as above except add 1 small pickling chili pepper, 1 teaspoon pickling spice, and 4 cloves garlic to each quart jar before sealing.

Dry Olives

dark, fully-ripened olives
rock salt

Place a layer of rock salt on the bottom of a wooden or cardboard container. Spread a layer of olives over this, then another layer of rock salt. Repeat until all olives have been used. Shake container each day. Olives are cured after 1 week. Remove olives from salt and put into jars. If you are not going to use olives within 2 months, place them under refrigeration. These olives go well with stews made of lamb, goat, or venison.

Pickled Cucumbers

   whole cucumbers 3-5 inches long
1   stalk green dill
2   tablespoons mustard seed
4   red pickling chili peppers
6   cloves garlic
¼   teaspoon alum
4   tablespoons salt
1   part cold vinegar (about 2½ cups)
2   parts cold water (about 5 cups)

Pack cucumbers in a gallon jar. Place dill, mustard seed, peppers, garlic, alum and salt in jar along with cucumbers. Boil vinegar with water; pour into jar and seal. Let stand 3 weeks.

Coccola or Italian Mushrooms

1½   cups mushrooms
3   tablespoons oil
2   tablespoons butter
1   clove garlic, chopped or pressed
¼   cup tomato sauce
¼   cup August Sebastiani Chablis
    or Country Chardonnay
    grated Parmesan cheese

Cut mushrooms into pieces and boil about 20 minutes. Drain well. Sauté mushrooms in oil and butter in frying pan. Add garlic, tomato sauce and wine. When mushrooms are cooked, add cheese as desired, stir once, and serve. Serves 3-4.

Baked Oyster Mushrooms

Mushrooms
chopped parsley
chopped garlic
salt
pepper
oregano
bread crumbs
olive oil

Wash mushrooms thoroughly and drain well. Place in single layers on cookie sheet and sprinkle generously with remaining ingredients. Bake in top of oven at 350 degrees until moisture is absorbed. If browning is desired, place under broiler for a few minutes and watch carefully so that mushrooms do not burn.

The quantity of mushrooms in this recipe is optional. Use condiments to suit your taste.

Cured Green Olives

1   gallon green olives, picked in autumn
    when olives first begin to get color
    and prior to first frost
5   ozs. lye
1½   lbs. salt
    water

Place olives in stone crock. Do not use any metal container. Mix lye with 2 gallons water and pour over olives. Use caution when handling lye as it is very caustic. Let olives stand 18 hours in this solution. Then pour off lye water again exercising caution, and wash olives until water is clear. Cover olives with 2 gallons water and ½ lb. salt. After 24 hours, drain olives again and cover with 2 gallons water and ½ lb. salt. Soak another 24 hours and repeat procedure. At end of third day, pack olives in jars, covering with brine. Keep refrigerated and wash with clear water before serving.

Stale Bread Fritters

5 slices stale bread, crusts removed
½ cup flour
½ cup milk
1 egg
1 teaspoon baking powder
½ teaspoon salt
4 tablespoons sugar
1 teaspoon cinnamon

Mix flour, milk, egg, baking powder, and salt into a batter. Cut each slice of bread into 4 long pieces. Dip bread into batter and fry in hot deep fat; drain well. Sprinkle with sugar and cinnamon.

Banana Fritters

1 cup flour
1 teaspoon baking powder
½ teaspoon salt
½-¾ cup milk
1 egg, well-beaten
1 tablespoon rum (optional)
1 or 2 ripe bananas
   sugar

Sift flour, baking powder, and salt. Add milk and egg and beat well. Skin and scrape the bananas; cut in half lengthwise, then across, making 4 pieces. Drop into batter and lift out with fork (do not pierce). Fry in hot deep fat and drain well when nicely browned. Sprinkle liberally with sugar.

Oven Roasted Chestnuts

2 lbs. chestnuts
3 tablespoons cooking oil
3 tablespoons August Sebastiani Country Cabernet Sauvignon or Zinfandel

With a sharp knife, carefully cut a ½ inch gash on either side of the shells of chestnuts. Heat oil in a heavy skillet and add chestnuts. Shake over heat for 5 minutes. Roast in 450 degree oven for another 5-10 minutes. When cooked, cover chestnuts with a cloth that has been soaked in wine. Allow to stand 5 minutes and serve.

Spiced Nuts

2½ cups walnut halves
1 cup sugar
1 teaspoon salt
1 teaspoon cinnamon
⅓ cup milk
1 teaspoon vanilla

Spread walnuts in shallow pan and roast for 20 minutes at 275 degrees. Remove as soon as nuts are cool enough to handle. Rub between hands, removing as much brown skin as possible. In saucepan, combine sugar, salt, cinnamon, and milk. Heat, stirring until sugar is dissolved. Boil until a few drops form a ball in cold water. Remove from heat and stir in vanilla. Add cooled walnuts and stir gently until creamy. Turn out onto waxed paper and separate nuts. Makes about 1 lb.

Sugared Nuts

3 cups almonds or walnuts
1 cup sugar
2 tablespoons honey
¼ cup water

If you use almonds, blanch and toast them. It is not necessary to do this to the walnuts. Combine sugar, honey, and water in a saucepan and cook until a few drops form a ball in cold water. Add nuts and stir until creamy. Separate the nuts and allow to cool. Makes about 1 lb.

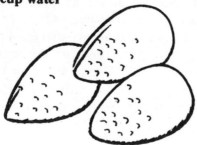

Sherried Walnuts

1¾ cup brown sugar, packed
¼ teaspoon salt
¼ cup Dry Sherry
2 tablespoons light corn syrup
3 cups walnut halves
  granulated sugar

Blend brown sugar, salt, sherry, and corn syrup. Stir in walnut halves, mixing until well-coated. Drop walnuts into granulated sugar and roll around until they have absorbed as much sugar as possible. Place on waxed paper to dry. Makes about 4 cups.

Cooked Prunes (No-Cook Way)

Cover prunes with boiling water, then cover with lid, and allow to cool. Let soak for 24 hours in the refrigerator. The longer the prunes soak, the more plump they will get.

Spiced Prunes

2   cups prunes
1   cinnamon stick
3   slices lemon
⅓   cup Tawny Port
     water

Combine all ingredients and cover completely with water. Cover and bring to a boil, then let simmer for about 15 minutes. Remove from heat, cool and refrigerate. The longer the prunes soak, the tastier they will be.

Canning or Preserving Italian Mushrooms (Moretti)

Proceed with caution before using the following recipes for mushrooms. Mushrooms can be very dangerous. If you are not expert in knowing your mushroom varieties, leave them alone.

       **mushrooms thoroughly washed
       and cut into pieces**
1   **part distilled vinegar to
       2 parts water**
1 or 2 **cloves garlic**
1 or 2 **tablespoons mixed
       pickling spices
       dried oregano
       salt**
1 or 2 **red chili peppers
       olive oil**

The amount of liquid used in this recipe depends on the amount of mushrooms. Use enough liquid to cover all mushrooms well. Bring liquid to boil with salt. Place garlic and spices into a piece of cloth and tie securely so that it can be easily removed before canning procedure. Add this cloth bag to boiling water, then add mushrooms and let boil 1 hour. Drain well and spread out on turkish towel for 24 hours. Put mushrooms into sterile pint jars, add 1 or 2 red chili peppers to each jar and fill with olive oil.

Another method for preparing mushrooms is to boil them as above and place them into jars, adding the boiled liquid and any spices you prefer. Top with a little olive oil and seal as if you were canning fruit. The mushrooms, along with their liquid, can also be put into milk cartons and placed in the freezer.

Brandy Sauce

1   cup water
¾   cup sugar
¼   cup butter
½   teaspoon salt
1   teaspoon grated orange
     peel (optional)
1   tablespoon cornstarch
     dissolved in 1 tablespoon
     cold water
2   tablespoons brandy

Mix all ingredients except brandy together and cook 5-10 minutes until mixture thickens. Add brandy, stir, and serve.

Raw Cranberry Sauce

1   package cranberries
1   large orange, whole and unpeeled
2   apples, unpeeled
2½   cups sugar

Chop or grind cranberries. Remove seeds from orange and core apples. Grind orange, apples, and cranberries together, then add sugar. Put into covered jars and refrigerate. Sauce freezes extremely well.

Hard Sauce

¼   cup butter
1   cup powdered sugar
1   teaspoon brandy

Cream butter, add sugar gradually, then add brandy. Use as a sauce over steamed puddings. If you prefer a thinner sauce, add more brandy.

Tomato Sauce

2   tablespoons olive oil
½   cup onion, finely chopped
2   cups solid pack tomatoes, chopped
     liquid from tomatoes
6   tablespoons tomato sauce
1   tablespoon fresh basil or 1
     teaspoon dried basil
1   teaspoon sugar
½   teaspoon salt
¼   teaspoon pepper

Heat oil in a saucepan; add onions and cook over moderate heat 7-8 minutes, until they are soft but not brown. Add tomatoes, tomato sauce, basil, sugar, salt, and pepper. Reduce heat to a low simmer, covering pan partially, and let cook 40 minutes, stirring occasionally. Season to taste.

Pickled Tomatoes

green tomatoes or cherry tomatoes
  three-fourths mature
few carrots, sliced into ¾ in. rounds
several celery stalks, sliced
cauliflower
small white onions, peeled

Follow same recipe as given for pickling cucumbers, but add carrots, celery, cauliflower, and onions to jars along with tomatoes.

Wine Jelly

2   cups any dry Sebastiani Wine, White,
    Red or Rosé
3   cups sugar
½   bottle fruit pectin
    paraffin

Put wine in top of double boiler. Add sugar and mix well. Place over rapidly boiling water and heat until wine is hot and sugar dissolved, stirring constantly. Remove from water at once and stir in pectin. Pour quickly into glasses and cover with paraffin at once. Makes 5-6 ounce glasses.

I recommend Sebastiani Chenin Blanc, Rosa Gewurztraminer, Zinfandel or Barbera for use in this recipe.

Zucchini Relish

2   quarts ground zucchini
4   medium white onions
1   large red bell pepper
     salted water
Vinegar sauce:
1½   cups sugar
2½   cups white vinegar
1   teaspoon tumeric
¼   teaspoon powdered cloves
1   teaspoon mustard

Remove seeds and soft pulp from zucchini. Grind zucchini, onions, and bell pepper together. Place in a pot and cover with salted water. Let stand 4 hours then drain well. Make vinegar sauce by boiling all ingredients together until spices are dissolved. Put in drained zucchini, onions, and pepper and bring to a second boil, stirring well. Fill pint jars and seal.

145

"WINE IN COOKING"

As you will note in my recipes, I use a lot of wine in cooking. It gives a flavor to certain dishes that cannot be had otherwise—many types of food would be bland and flat without it. The flavor in wine is due to the nature of wine and not the alcohol. The alcohol escapes during cooking and none is present in the finished dish.

An all purpose wine for cooking is a good sound dry white wine—such as Chablis, Chardonnay or Sauvignon Blanc. The dry red wines are good, but they present a problem as they will darken certain dishes. They are compatible to dishes like stews, minestrone and certain types of roast meats. I use and recommend a fresh bottle of wine for cooking, but a partly full bottle can be kept in the refrigerator for a week for cooking purposes.

Many of my friends use varying amounts of wine in recipes similar to mine—this is all a matter of experience and personal preference.

"WINE IN OUR FAMILY"

I grew up in a family where wine was part of our everyday living. It was just as much a part of mealtime as salt and pepper. A lunch or a dinner without wine would not seem right. I recall that my father-in-law's dad, old Lorenzo, would absolutely refuse to sit down for his meal unless a bottle of wine was already on the table. If he did not have his glass of wine or two with his meal we knew he was not well, which was not often as he lived to be 94. In spite of the presence of wine at all meals, temperance prevailed. Wine was always treated with respect as a part of our life. It was even given to the young—diluted with water.

If you went to visit one of the old-timers and he offered you some of his favorite wine, you would have insulted him not to at least take a taste of it. During prohitition most of the farmers that we knew made their own wines, and each one thought his wine was better than his neightbor's. They made wine with pride, treated it with care, and their wine cellar was a very important part of their home. I recall one time when my husband bought a piece of farmland from an old Frenchman, part of the consideration he had to make to his old friend was that he would furnish him with a gallon of wine per week for the balance of his life.

On cold winter nights a visit to a friend's home would often bring out hot roasted chestnuts and a good bottle of red wine. Many were the Sunday afternoons I would see some of the men sit out under a tree in the backyard with an ice bucket and some good white wine, sipping the time away.

Today the basement homemade wine is pretty much a thing of the past. However, wine is still there, but it is wine made by others. In my home I have a large assortment of red and white wines, as well as sherries, ports, champagne, and a few bottles of dry and sweet vermouth. With the exception of breakfast, wine is available with all meals. When I have company, I often serve wine before lunch or dinner in place of cocktails.

I have found that I get a great deal of satisfaction in knowing that I always have a few bottles of our special vintages or special bin selections put away for those extra special occasions. I am sure that you will find too that by having some of these special wines put away they will become the highlight of any meal.

I have enjoyed many different wines over the years with many combinations of meals. The following is more than just a description of what wines to use with what foods, but is intended as a little glossary on the proper approach to wines.

STORAGE

All bottles of wine should be kept lying down so that the corks remain moist to keep them from drying out and permitting air to come into contact with the contents. Air is the prime enemy of wine, and keeping the cork wet prohibits air's entry into the bottle. Dessert wines are an exception to this rule. Due to their higher alcohol, deterioration is prevented, and these wines, therefore, may be stored with the neck up.

The temperature of storage should be as even as possible the year around, and the ideal is from 50 to 55 degrees F. Always store your Champagne nearest the floor, then your still whites, and on top your still reds. If you are going to use a binning cellar, a bin that permits selection of any bottle is usually the best, so that you don't have to disturb others to take one.

GLASSWARE

All glasses should be clear in order to show the brilliancy in color of their contents. In opaque or tinted glass the color of the wine is changed. They should be as thin as possible and should be tulip-shaped with the upper rim turning inwards in order to direct the aroma and bouquet to your nose. Metal goblets should not be used for wine service, as they do not do justice to their contents. They do not allow observance of the true color of the wine and, in most cases, seem to give a metallic flavor to the wine.

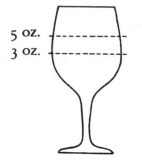

5 oz.

3 oz.

A good all-purpose wine glass is a clear, stemmed 6-9 oz. capacity glass. You can use it to serve all wines, including sparkling and dessert wines. For table and sparkling wines fill to about 5 ounces. For dessert and appetizer wines fill with 2-3 ounces.

If you prefer, however, you can obtain 2½ to 4 oz., tulip-shaped dessert wine glasses for both appetizer and dessert wines; tulip-shaped 9 oz; glasses for dinner wines; and champagne glasses for sparkling wines. The champagne glasses are of 5 oz. capacity and can either be tulip or saucer shaped.

TABLE SETTING

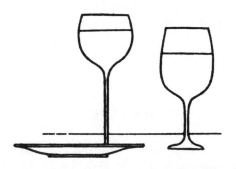

Wine glasses are usually placed at the right. If more than one wine is to be served, the glass for the first wine is placed the farthest to the right. If you are serving an elaborate meal, no more than three wine glasses should be in front of each guest at any time. Remove used glasses as each course is finished.

SERVING TEMPERATURES

The proper temperature of serving wine is for Champagne at about 35 degrees F. This can be obtained by putting the Champagne in a pail of cracked ice for an hour, or putting it in the cold part of the refrigerator for about an hour. White still wines, such as Chablis, Chenin Blanc, Sauvignon Blanc, Johannisberg Riesling, Gewurztraminer, Chardonnay, should be at about 50 degrees F. This would be about 30 minutes in cracked ice or about an hour and a half in the refrigerator, and they may be served immediately after opening. Replace the cork after each serving. Rosé wines should be treated and served as the white wines.

Still red wines, such as, Burgundy, Gamay Beaujolais, Zinfandel, Barbera, Cabernet Sauvignon, Pinot Noir, should be served at 65° to 70° F. (Room temperature.) Stand the bottle up for a couple hours in your dining room before serving. This will bring the red wine up to the temperature of the room. It will also allow any sediment to settle to the bottom of the bottle. Remember the correct temperatures bring out the beauties of wines; incorrect temperatures prevent justice to you and your guests and hide the aromas and delicate flavors which you may expect. Do not replace the cork once the serving has begun. Naturally, it should be replaced when the wine is to be put away for a day or so of storage.

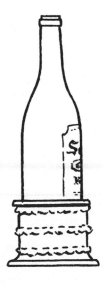

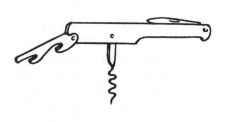

The proper method of opening and serving wines would be as follows for Champagne. Always hold the bottle so it is pointed in a *safe* direction. That is, away from anyone's face. At the proper temperature, wipe the bottle dry, break the loop on the wire hood by bending from side to side, remove the wire and the top of the foil cap, which is usually perforated. Hold the cork firmly with the left hand, use a napkin if preferred, twist the bottle with the right hand holding it at the bottom of the bottle. When the cork turns in the bottle, continue to twist the bottle until you feel the cork rising.

Then try to keep the cork from coming out too quickly. Ease it out, so as to let the gas escape gradually. During the whole operation use great care to keep the bottle at rest, for agitating it releases the gas, and in consequence the effervescence will not remain as long in the glass. Carefully wipe off the inside of the mouth of the bottle. When pouring, do not wrap the bottle in a napkin, but have one in the left hand under the bottle to catch either the sweat of the bottle (caused by its being cold) or a drip from the bottle falling on the tablecloth. As you finish pouring into a glass, twist the bottle as you bring the mouth of the bottle up. This avoids most drippage.

For all still wines (non-sparkling), when they have been brought to the proper temperature, cut off the top of the lead foil just below the lip. Stand the bottle on a flat surface and hold it firmly. Insert the corkscrew in the middle of the cork, screw it down straight, so that the end of the corkscrew will be below the bottom of the cork.

Pull slowly and carefully so as not to shake the bottle. I recommend a lever corkscrew as used by sommeliers in the better restaurants.

Wipe the inside of the mouth of the bottle and pour with napkin as for Champagne.

Many gourmet shops have wine coasters available in which your bottle may be placed while not in use. These are decorative on the table, as well as practical for keeping linen tablecloths clean. Also available are bottle collars used to stop any drippage from reaching the base of the bottle. These too are quite attractive and add to the conversation value of the wine served.

DECANTING

All still wines that have been bottled a year or more are likely to throw some sediment. The deeper colored, full-bodied red wines having more than the lighter wines. This comes from the natural development of the wine, but it must be allowed to settle to the bottom before the wine is used, otherwise it detracts from the flavor. This sediment has a coarse and bitter taste. To serve, stand the bottle upright for a few days before using. A good way to always be prepared is to keep one or two bottles standing up. A month in this position will not hurt them, as the cork will stay wet that long. Draw the cork carefully, as described above, and then by preference decant.

In order to do this, merely pour slowly into the preferred decanter until you see the first sediment coming out of the lip of the bottle. Have a light behind the bottle so that you can see when the sediment begins to rise. Stop pouring just before the sediment would go into the decanter. Serve from the decanter. If you serve from the bottle, pour very slowly and fill all the glasses without turning the bottle upright, so as not to dislodge the sediment from the bottom of the bottle.

We have observed over the years that it is to the benefit of a red wine to open it an hour before the meal and leave the cork off. If it is a wine which requires decanting, it is preferable to let it breathe after decanting. The purpose of this breathing is to allow some of the more volatile unpleasant odors, such as cork smell, to dissipate as well as allow the air to soften the wine.

When serving—pour slowly and with ceremony.

WHAT WINES WITH WHAT FOODS

To cover this subject is not easy, but these are our recommendations. Every food has a complementary drink, and the correct combination brings out the full qualities and flavors of each. Before the meal a Champagne serves to stimulate one's appetite, relax any tensions of the day, and begin the evening with the connoisseur's touch. This also gives the cook time to let everyone arrive before putting on the last minute dishes.

With the meal, white wines, such as Chablis, Chenin Blanc, Johannisberg Riesling, Gewurztraminer, Chardonnay, can be served with oysters, soup, fish and white meats and at luncheons with the lighter dishes that are normally served mid-day.

Rosés and "blush" wines, such as White Zinfandel or "Eye of the Swan" Pinot Noir Blanc, can be served either with foods recommended for white wines, or, if you desire, with foods recommended for reds. These wines are intended to please as intermediate wines of medium body and flavors and have the widest range of uses. Serve Burgundy, Gamay Beaujolais, Zinfandel, Barbera, Cabernet Sauvignon, Pinot Noir with red meats, game, all cheese—but not with oysters or fish.

Champagne can be served all through a meal after the soup and fish. Champagne is suitable at all times and goes with all foods. It is essential for weddings, wedding breakfasts, anniversaries, reunions, celebrations, and can be served after dinner all through the evening. When a variety of wines are served at one meal, if possible, serve the lighter types first (generally the whites first), leading up to the heavier wines. There is a definite reason for this, as the heavier-bodied red wines will dull your taste buds for the more delicate white wines.

After the meal a Tawny Port or the Cream Sherry with nuts or cheese make a fitting ending to any evening where enjoyment of food is primary. Don't overlook the use of either Dry Vermouth or Sweet Vermouth over ice as an appetizer before the meal.

I hope I have not disappointed you in my brief allocation of wines to food. I believe that you will find, as we have, that as you taste various wines you will find one, or maybe two wines, that you especially prefer. This then should be your rule, drink what you like with whatever foods you prefer. For example, if you settle on a Chardonnay, as I have, you will find that it goes quite well with steaks. I would not recommend a red wine with oysters, but my husband often drank it with some preparations of fish and wild fowl, such as duck. He preferred the red wines to white and drank them almost exclusively.

Below I have drawn up a glossary of the wines Sebastiani produces and the foods with which they are ideally suited. This will serve as a starting point for you, but when you find a wine you like don't concern yourself about the rules—let your palate be the judge—if you enjoy it with a dish, drink it.

Red Wines

Barbera
Burgundy
Cabernet Sauvignon
Gamay Beaujolais
Pinot Noir
Zinfandel

Best with Hearty Dishes

Steaks, Roasts
Cheese, Stews
Game, Spaghetti
Casseroles, Chops

Rosé and Blush Wines

"Eye of the Swan" Pinot Noir Blanc
"Rosa" Gewurztraminer
Vin Rosé
White Zinfandel

Ham, Pork
Veal, Lamb
Poultry

White Wines

Chablis
Chardonnay
Chenin Blanc
French Colombard
Gewurztraminer
Johannisberg Riesling
Sauvignon Blanc or Fumé Blanc

Poultry, Soups
Fruits, Fruit Salads
Fish
Shellfish

Appetizer Wines

Champagne or Sparkling Wine

Soup

COMPARING WINES

At this point some notes on tasting and judging wines may be of interest. It is impossible to taste any beverage fairly if you have previously formed an opinion of it. Try to be as unprejudiced as possible. If you ask friends to pass judgement, do not let them know what they are tasting, and try to avoid imparting any hint of your opinion whether good or bad. Before tasting, be sure that the wine in the glass is of the proper temperature, that you have the correct glass, and if there is any sediment that it has settled to the bottom of the bottle. The glass should not be more than one-quarter full. Look for soundness, cleanness and something that will give you pleasure to drink. We believe that if one glass invites the second, the wine is good.

In judging wines, look first for brilliancy, a characteristic known to tasters as candle-bright. Second, look for perfect color. Is it correct for the type you are tasting? If it is sparkling wine, judge for effervescence. The bubbles should be very small, constantly rising and breaking the surface. Smell the wine. Swing the glass with a rotary motion so as to release the esters. Put your nose over the middle of the glass and inhale deeply. It should smell clean. There should be no sign of yeast or of incomplete fermentation. No woody, corky, or casky smell, or doubtful aroma. The aroma should be completely homogenious. It should be a single unit, not two or more distinct smells. You should detect a delicate bouquet, and you should note the characteristics of the particular type you are tasting.

Next, taste it. This is the final test. Take a small quantity in your mouth and roll it around so as to cover the four groups of tasting glands on your tongue. One on the tip, one on each side, and one on the back, just in front of your palate. Look first for cleanness, second for sweetness or acidity. Distinguish between acidity and sourness. Don't conclude it as sour if it is simply dry. Sourness means the presence of acetic acid vinegar. Third, look for body. Is it thin and watery, or does it fill your mouth with flavor? Is the general impression pleasing? The answer to this question is most important.

And then last, is it true to type? In every type there are decided differences in flavor, bouquet, and other characteristics. You cannot condemn a Chenin Blanc because it is not like a Chardonnay. Yet they are both perfect types of wines in spite of their pronounced different individualities. Slowly sip a small glass and get your impression of the aftertaste. It should be clean and pleasant and create the desire for another glass. After that, smell the empty glass. If there are any defects they will appear.

INDEX